Loving Emma

by the same author

We Became Like a Hand
A Story of Five Sisters

Loving Emma

A Story
of Reluctant
Motherhood

CAROL A. ORTLIP

alyson books
NEW YORK

Author's Note: This is a work of nonfiction; some names have been changed out of respect for those who experienced life differently from the way I may have documented it here.

Manufactured in the United States of America

This trade paperback original is published by Alyson Books
245 West 17th Street, New York, NY 10011

Distribution in the United Kingdom by
Turnaround Publisher Services Ltd.
Unit 3, Olympia Trading Estate, Coburg Road, Wood Green,
London N22 6TZ England

First Edition: July 2008

08 09 10 11 12 13 14 15 16 17 a 10 9 8 7 6 5 4 3 2 1

ISBN: 1-59350-065-3
ISBN-13: 978-1-59350-065-8

Library of Congress Cataloging-in-Publication data are on file.

Cover design by Victor Mingovits

For Emma, of course
And for Gemma, the love of my life

CONTENTS

ACKNOWLEDGMENTS

To my team at I.N.S.P.I.R.E for Autism: Stephanie Betit, Kathleen Vranos, Bill Vranos, Craig White, Bob Johnson, and Gordon Bristol. Our new venture is creating hope and a new vision for our community. Thanks for believing in me and the dream.

Everyone at Westminster Center School.

My father, Paul Daniel Ortlip. May 1926–February 2008.

Basia, the dream dog.

My sisters, Kate and Michele Ortlip.

Richard Fumosa, the most understanding editor from Alyson Books, who deserves an award for his patience and support.

Linda Konner, my agent, whom I love and adore with devotion.

Gemma. Where would I be without you?

Emma. You are showing me the way.

Loving Emma

PROLOGUE

Emma is harnessed wild energy channeled into her project. Her room is a flourish of colors, shapes, and motion as she ignites paper, scissors, markers, glue, wood, aluminum foil, and pieces of cloth into creation after creation, all of which she must present to us. For a little while she is silent, every bit of focus is directed into her hands, those long, slender fingers translating imagination into the world of dimension.

Partially eaten pieces of a grilled cheese sandwich lie next to her, evidence that she has eaten something at least. I swear, if we didn't bring her food at required intervals or remind her to feed herself, I'm not sure she would. She gets hungry, of that we're sure, but she becomes so intensely involved with the activity in her hands that the sensation of hunger doesn't seem to register in a place of immediate cognition. This myopic single-mindedness seems to cut off her need for food, drink, or rest; we must make sure she gets them.

As with most children like Emma, when pushed to attend to tasks she doesn't want to do or that are difficult for her, this super-ability to block out everything except what's right in front of her disappears. We fight with her to get homework done. In the thick of fifth grade (yes, an important year in the acquisition of academic knowledge), those of us who teach and parent her are ready to alleviate her suffering and ours by doing away with homework except for twenty minutes of reading a night. The struggles are just not worth the return: half-completed, sometimes sloppy, tear-stained math and spelling assignments.

What do we hold her to? This creative, impulsive, complex, wired, pre-adolescent we have been called upon to raise. For Emma is not my child nor does she "belong" to Gemma, my life partner since 1991. She comes from Tanya, Gemma's younger sister, who, in 2003, delivered Emma to us in a desperate attempt to save her from the hell into which Tanya was descending. Cocaine had reclaimed Tanya's life and she didn't want it to ruin Emma's life, too. Was giving Emma to us a purely selfless act? I don't believe it was. For Tanya knew that Gemma and I could never turn away from Emma, whom we had known since birth. Tanya knew we'd raise her with as much competency and love as we could muster. She knew that entrusting her daughter to us would ensure Emma's safe passage through to a time when they could be together again in some capacity.

And now, six years later, Tanya and Emma are able to have a relationship. With Tanya on the mend, clean for years, married to a sweet, supportive guy, and singing hymns every Sunday at the church to which she belongs, they are happily through the worst and into the kind of relationship I wish I had had with my mother.

But this story is not about Emma and Tanya's relationship—not directly. It is about my relationships: with Gemma, with Emma, but mostly with myself. This story is about rising to an unplanned responsibility. It is about huge, cavernous doubt. Troubling behaviors. Falling from grace. Resistance of the highest order. The opening to shared laughter and joy. It is about staying the course. It is about growing up rather late in life.

This is a story for anyone who has been asked to take on a family member's child, for whatever the reason. This is a story about learning to love all over again, and in ways unimaginable. This is a story about learning to love a girl named Emma.

1

FIST FIRST

*E*mma was born fist first, straight up and out, rising from an incision sliced down her mother's lower abdomen. After twenty-seven hours of labor, a Caesarian was the only option. Emma's vital signs were slowing down to the point of no return and Tanya was too exhausted to continue pushing. Clearly, through the vaginal canal and out into the light of midday was not the route Emma could take and survive.

Gemma, my partner, Tanya's older sister and Emma's namesake, was there to see the clenched right hand emerge first. Out it came: little fist. Little fighter. Little bird. Little last ray of hope for Tanya.

Did the appearance of this little fist mean Emma was here to fight for her mother's life? Save her? Keep her away from cocaine, the dark side? Did the rising fist mean Emma was here simply to fight for her own life and her own right to it? If Tanya was going to turn her life around, get clean and find a reason to stay clean, certainly the birth of her daughter was a most compelling reason to try. Whether Emma was here to fight for herself, or her mother, ultimately does not matter in the grand scheme of things. Emma was here, emerging fist first. Some kind of a fight had begun for each of us who would figure prominently in her life. Fights of loyalty. Fights with the cunning and conniving devil of resistance. Fights that began, renewed, and ended relationships. And some fights that may never be called "resolved."

Gemma and I had been together for more than five years when Emma was born. Partnered, we had already been through the death of my sister Danielle from leukemia, relocation from Burlington, Vermont, to a smaller village in the southern part of the state, and the acquisition of our dog, Basia. Our relationship seemed solid, from as many angles as I could find. But, of course, I wasn't looking at it from the angle of potential parent. The birth of Emma did not arouse that thought in me, even when I heard Gemma tell the spirit of the baby before she was born to skip this life—and, if she couldn't, to skip over her if she was looking for any kind of help. I should have figured out that Gemma was already thinking about the possibility of our becoming parents to her sister's child. Why wouldn't she think of this? Some things are set in crystal and from whatever facet you approach it, a crystal it is. Right from the moment of conception, Emma was beginning to move toward us, despite the beliefs and desires of everyone around her and despite something called denial.

Once Emma was safely established at home in Florida with Tanya, well over her very first bout of projectile puking (an allergic reaction to soy-based baby formula), looking healthy and sufficiently doted upon, Gemma flew back to Vermont. Before she left, Gemma made Tanya promise to call if she felt herself slipping toward an urge to use or if she felt like sliding toward the need to see Sam.

Emma was born in October; the first SOS rang through in December. Speaking to a storm-trooping Gemma was not enough to stop Tanya from using again. By the beginning of January, Tanya and Emma were on a plane bound for New England. We picked them up and brought them to our drafty farmhouse in Vermont, where they would live until an opening at a local substance-abuse family program became available. It was obviously going to be like this now: Everything we do is for the baby. But the baby did not come by herself. Standing, lying, sitting, crouching, and trying to be as unobtrusive as possible right next to said baby was Tanya, at all times. She was just the kind of houseguest I wanted living with us. Not. From two women with a dog, we went to two women with a dog, a drug addict, and her three-month-old baby. It wasn't just the shock of their sudden arrival that kept me in a perpetual state of silent bewilderment; it was watching Gemma move right into guardian and stage manager roles without so much as twitching an eyebrow. Sure, she asked me if I was OK with it all. Looking into her determined eyes, countenance of an admiral and hands at the ready, I didn't think I had any other choice. And, in fact, if I had objected to their sudden arrival, I am sure that Gemma would have convinced me to change my mind either by using an intelligent, persuasive presentation of rational and heart-felt reasons or by using a strong-arm approach. I could clearly see that if I refused to allow Tanya and Emma to live with us until "we" found a suitable rehabilitation facility for them, the result would be a swift and ugly conflict with Gemma. I will avoid conflict at any cost. I would take in Gemma's entire family before I would let a conflict erupt. And so, I thought, *OK. I can do this. What kind of inconvenience could possibly come from letting Tanya and Emma live with us for a while? I mean, for Pete's sake?*

Tanya and Emma are asleep in the upstairs guest room. This box of a room is not well insulated, rendering it as close to a refrigerator as a room can get and for a baby, probably not the best place for sleeping. We searched the house for as many space heaters as we could and then surrounded the double bed with them. These heaters are on all the time since Tanya and Emma spend a lot of their waking and sleeping hours upstairs together in bed. It's the beginning of their intense bonding phase—a phase that helped to establish a lasting need in Emma to always have someone lying next to her as she falls asleep.

Tanya and Emma are very sweet together, I must admit. There is plenty of mommy/baby wrestling—Emma grabbing at Tanya's face, holding her nose, pulling on her wild hair, sticking her fingers into her mouth. Tanya clearly loves it, her face a revolving canvas of adoring expressions. I watch and wonder. Why doesn't this relationship keep Tanya from wanting to use drugs?

Tanya stumbles down the stairs after spending over an hour getting Emma to sleep. She is spent, looking for something. A treat? A moment of rest? A cup of tea? A cigarette? That will have to do. I watch her standing outside under the eaves that barely protect her from the elements: snow and wind. She is huddled up, collar of her bathrobe raised against the cold. She can't light the cigarette. Over and over she tries but the wind keeps blowing out the flame of the lighter. I knock on the window and motion her into the mudroom.

"Tanya. Just light it in here," I offer.

"But I don't want to get any smoke . . ."

"It's all right. Go ahead." I try making it easier for her.

"Thanks, Carol." She looks relieved.

She lights it and then steps back outside, inhaling as often as every five seconds. There are no breaks in the inhalations and exhalations until the cigarette is down to the filter. She comes into the mudroom, lights another cigarette, and goes outside again. She finishes the second one as quickly as the first, comes in, hangs up the sweater she has thrown over her shoulders, smiles meekly at me, and tiptoes back upstairs. Maybe I should have asked her to sit down, have a cup of something warm, and talk awhile. I am not sure why I didn't but I am not ready to spend any time figuring it out. It's enough that I am slowly opening myself to the growing feelings of adoration for this baby. Each passing day brings Emma closer and closer, her little baby face and hands looking for my big face and smile. As soon as I see her, I smile; I can't help it. And now she starts laughing as soon as she sees me. She literally goes into a belly laugh, unless she is so tired that she doesn't have the energy for it. Sometimes she stretches out her arms to me and I put her to sleep with a Celtic tape my sister Kate sent me. This new routine started by accident a week or so ago. Kate heard that Tanya was having a hard time putting Emma down for naps so she made a copy of a tape she used with her daughter, Anna. One afternoon, when Tanya was wiped out from trying, she handed Emma off to me and went back upstairs to sleep alone. I hollowed out the space right in front of my heart and took Emma into my arms. She touched my face and looked into my eyes.

"It's you and me, little bubblehead," I whispered. Her face turned toward the window as I inserted the tape into the machine. I set the volume and lowered the lights. With an almost imperceptible sigh, Emma pushed down in and closer. Her left eye was running, the small tear duct clogged up with encrusted salt water; soon she would need surgery to keep it from running. She looked out through the yellowing liquid without complaint. After about ten minutes, she was barely awake, the Celtic melodies, the rocking, the sleet rapping gently against the window, were all conspiring to lower her resistance.

It wasn't long before she was asleep and I had taken all of

her weight into me. I continued to rock her, listening to the music, aware of the fading daylight left on the small apple tree just outside the kitchen window. I looked at Emma's face, a little stain of tear water visible, oozing off from the corner of her eye. I wiped it away as softly as I could so as not to rouse her. Her lips pursed into a smile. I loved her so much at that moment, I couldn't move; I was frozen fully into this feeling of love for her.

"I'll always be here for you, Emma. I promise. Remember this."

I smelled the top of her head, sweet, warm, and delicate, like the scent of Lily of the Valley bells coming in through an open window during those early days of spring. Then I walked her back upstairs, returning her into the arms of her mother.

I am home from work earlier than usual. There's some kind of cold front moving in; I've got to make the house warm for everyone before night comes. I like having the wood stove cranking so the living room is warm enough for Emma to play in comfortably.

Gemma is on the phone; she raises a finger to her lips, points at the receiver, and then points upstairs. I've got to be quiet on two fronts: Tanya and Emma must be asleep and whoever is on the other end of the phone isn't napping but it must be an important call. So I nod, find our dog, the Basia girl, and head outside for a romp in the snow. Our five-year-old black Labrador/Australian sheepdog mix loves the snow as much as I do. I can't wait to watch her leap out into it, like it's the first time she's ever seen snow. Basia jumps face-first into snow—she reminds me of a fox I once spotted in a field above the house where I lived at the time. The fox must have been after a field mouse or mole, determining its location by tracking the rodent's scent. Once the fox had reached the spot, it pounced directly up and then, snout first, down into the hole of whatever creature it actually turned out to be. Over and over the fox put on this lithe and gravity-defiant display. I watched until the fox had a squirming ball of life clenched in its jaws. Without so much as a bow or curtsy, it fled up the field, to enjoy its meal in private, I assumed.

Basia, not after a rodent as far as I knew, performed similar acrobatics when set loose upon a snowy expanse, especially if the snow was deep or banked up into drifts. Her exuberance had been contagious enough on certain occasions to get me mimicking her. Once, side-by-side, we both dug our faces into a particularly tantalizing snowbank. With our faces planted, I turned to look at her. Wild, wet, black nose set vibrating into the white powder made me laugh so hard, I sucked in a huge mouthful of snow and fell backwards, choking. Basia jumped right onto me, licking my face with her cold, smooth tongue, helping me laugh. Always helping me laugh.

After our romp, Basia and I shake off in the mudroom. I wipe salt, snow, and sand from her sensitive paws. Ice mats up the fur in between the pads, sometimes causing her to slip and slide all over the wood floor.

Gemma is off the phone, sitting at the dining room table,

writing intently on a yellow legal pad. She looks up and smiles.

"I've got some good news. There's an opening."

At first I don't know what she is talking about. An opening? In what? The ozone layer? She wouldn't be smiling, would she?

"I just got off the phone with the family rehab place. Tanya and Emma can move in next week."

"Next week? That's really soon."

"I thought you wanted them to get going as soon as possible."

"Well, yeah, but that is really soon." I am as surprised as she is at my reaction.

"You're getting attached to them, too, huh?"

"Well, I wouldn't say attached to them. Attached to Emma." Gemma knows that my feelings for Tanya are not exactly tender ones.

"Do you want to hear about the program?"

"Sure." Why not?

For a year, Tanya and Emma lived in a small apartment building, which had three other units housing drug-addicted women and their children. For a year, Tanya attended classes on parenting, went to Narcotics Anonymous meetings just about every day, and took high school courses in order to get her GED. For a year, Gemma offered twenty-four-hour support. I watched as she became central operator of the Tanya-Get-Clean-Movement. She handled all paperwork, made all the phone calls and appointments, and filled in as babysitter whenever Tanya needed it. Gemma tried not to ask for my help unless absolutely necessary. Perhaps she knew that I would be called on later to step up to responsibilities that would be much more demanding than any I was capable of imagining then. Perhaps she knew that I was not ready for a commitment that would last a lifetime. Perhaps she knew that I was a slow and resistant learner, especially in areas I pretended I didn't understand.

Emma is dancing, if the swaying and rocking back and forth can be called dancing. I have never seen a two-year-old toddling child actually dance. They basically just shift their weight from one foot to the other, to a rhythm that rarely matches the beat of whatever song is playing. If they really get whipped up, they might start to spin and rock at the same time—Emma is not doing the spin but now she's trying to clap her hands, as well. Fingers spread back for maximum palm contact; one out of three attempts actually make it. With her tiny derriere sticking out behind her, she really does look very much like a spastic duck.

Her smile takes up most of her face. Emma would dance for hours if allowed and if the rest of us didn't become exhausted from taking turns dancing with her. She will dance alone, but Emma prefers a dancing partner; no one likes to dance alone.

We turn off the music. Tanya and Gemma flop back in the small sofa in the living room of the small apartment Tanya and Emma live in now. This one did not come furnished, as some of the apartments they have inhabited have been. Gemma and I helped them find furniture, well mostly Gemma, who has an in with the second-hand stores in southern Vermont because she works in one. This place is heading toward cozy: hooked rugs, worn-in chairs and couches, still-life acrylic paintings by Don (Gemma and Tanya's father), and Emma's flotilla of toys, books, movies, crayons, paper, and unidentified plastic objects—neither toy nor tool, these things serve only as clutter.

The location of this apartment is not great; it sits in the seedy side of town, a six unit, low income building housing welfare moms with or without kids and with or without men around. Tanya and Emma are safe enough here, we hope. Gemma and I are frequent visitors, Gemma almost daily. She is on watch for any signs of a Tanya relapse; Tanya is just months out of the family rehabilitation program. Here they are now, in Phase Two, trying to live a normal life.

My visits usually turn into playtimes with Emma. We've got a buddy relationship going—I'm a playmate—a rather large one but nevertheless, that's who I am for her. It's fine with me. I'd much rather play with Emma than yack around with Tanya; Gemma handles that with pure aplomb.

Once the music is turned off, Emma takes my hand and pulls me to the bedroom where she and Tanya sleep. The king-sized bed that Tanya purchased (the only purchase and one that seemed wastefully extravagant), takes up the entire room except for a slim space next to the right side of the bed— enough room for getting by, barely. We fall onto the bed together; the wrestling will now commence. We roll around all over each other, mostly with Emma on top of me. I hold her above me with my feet, playing Froggy Elevator. Emma laughs until she is foaming at the mouth, her spit falling into my face, in little globs. Hers is a belly laugh; for such a tiny child with what, I imagine to be, a tiny belly, she has a fairly deep one, coming in at the lower range in decibels and tone. It's startling to hear her laugh, especially if you're not expecting it. Turning to find an adult laughing and finding this pipsqueak, Emma, instead, can bust your hold on reality into bits. "That sound came out of her?"

We finally stop wrestling, tickling, laughing, and spitting. Sitting cross-legged on the bed, I wait to see what Emma wants to do next. She scuttles over to me, reaching for my long mane of hair. She loves my hair and loves when I gently whip it all over her face, strands tickling every inch. She doesn't giggle or laugh when I do this; she gets very quiet, almost meditative, the motion and feel of my hair putting her in some kind of trance-like state.

This time, she places her hands on my head and slowly pulls it down toward her. When my head is just about touching her head, she peers in at me, through my hair, smiles and methodically strokes my face in a much ritualized manner, taking care to do it just as if there was a pattern she must follow. She is quiet and intent, focused on, what seems to be, a job she is performing or an act of healing she knows I need. Gemma and Tanya walk in as Emma continues, her little fingers running through the same motions again and again. They stand transfixed; I know they are as curious as I am as to what Emma is doing exactly.

In a few more minutes, Emma is finished, jumping back up into a playful kid posture; she's ready for another round of Froggy Elevator.

"What do you think Emma was doing to me with those little hands of hers?" I ask Gemma on our way home later.

"Magic."

"I don't understand what you mean," I say.

"I know you don't. Maybe you will someday," she answers.

Staying near the people she met in rehab ultimately turned out to be a bad thing for Tanya and Emma, for the women in the program did not stand a good chance of staying clean. The recovery rate for drug-addicted women is some crazy percentage: maybe one in ten stay clean. Tanya's "network" of friends only leads her back to using and, eventually, back to Florida to try to live again with Sam. They had been corresponding all along, their letters fanciful, dream-filled pages of promises and plans. Gemma came home from their apartment one day with a face as puffed up and red as I had ever seen it. Her announcement was grim. Tanya was driving back to Florida in a month. She had decided to make a family with Sam and Emma; she owed it to Emma and to herself to have a normal life.

I didn't say a word. What world could ever be "normal" with Tanya in it?

Emma, Tanya, and Kay (Tanya and Gemma's mother) are standing near Tanya's car, which is packed with all the belongings Tanya could jam into it for the move back to Florida. Tanya and Emma don't have that much, these past years spent in furnished apartments. Kay flew up from Florida, where she lives, in order to make the trip with Tanya and Emma by car to help out with the care of Emma; she doesn't drive and never has.

Gemma and I stand together, trying hard not to cry and give in to our feelings of grief and dread. Neither one of us is supportive of Tanya's decision to move back to Florida, get back together with Sam once he's out of jail which will be in a month's time, and set up house with him and Emma. Gemma, who cannot keep her strong opinions to herself, has expressed her very rational misgivings to Tanya many times over the past month, since the decision was made. But Tanya will do what she wants; she claims to still love Sam, insists he's clean, as is she, and she wants to give their dream of a "regular" life together a fighting chance. The operative and suspicious word here is "fighting" because we are sure that a fight is what they are in for: either a fight of the knock-down-drag-out abusive sort, the futile, it-will-never-work sort, the get-two-drug-addicts-together-again sort or the you-were-right-all-along kind of fight. Tanya has been doing so well here in Vermont, we think, it's hard to see her leaving the place where her sobriety has remained strong.

We've already said goodbye to them but Emma wants to hug and kiss her "Gigi" and "Kiki" one more time. Tanya walks her back over to us and Emma falls into Gemma's arms for the squeeze. This proves to be too much for Gemma, who, as soon as she's holding Emma again, begins to sob. Emma pushes back from her and looks her in the face, her face animated with concern. She hugs Gemma again, patting her rhythmically on the back. I place my arms around both of them, offering what I can in the way of support. I do not cry, not now anyway. I want to be able to comfort Gemma during this impossible goodbye.

I can tell that Gemma is having a difficult time letting go of Emma, so I gently take Emma into my arms, giving her a brief hug myself and then giving her to Tanya. Kay has already gotten in the car; she waits patiently, holding a bedraggled-looking Kleenex to her face. Tanya straps Emma into the car seat behind the driver's seat, looks at us as she closes the door, promises to call us from their first hotel stop, gets in the car, and heads down the steep driveway. I embrace Gemma while she cries. We stay this way a long time, both of us probably asking ourselves the same question: How long will it be before the bad news comes?

Gemma is holding more tightly onto Emma than I have ever seen her. It is as though she is afraid that if she lets her go, Emma will vanish, becoming vapor, all traces of her earthly form gone in a flash. I don't say anything. I simply join in the embrace. We haven't seen her in months, the stories about Tanya's latest relapse and Sam's trip back to jail coming to us from Gemma's parents, Kay and Don. These constant reports have only served to feed our growing sense that the rescue call was imminent.

We're here to take Emma back to Vermont with us. A visit, an overnight, and then we'll fly back, with Tanya to follow once she is found (no one knows where she is), admitted to, and finishes another stay in rehab. We take her because we all know Tanya may not turn up for weeks. We take her because that is what Tanya would want and that is what Emma wants.

Gemma and I observe and examine Emma, looking for any signs of damage. If there are any, they are hidden, somewhere on the inside. We stay close to her that first night, never letting her go even a room away from us. Somehow, it seems too risky. Emma appears to be oblivious of her mother's absence, more than happy and now, occupied with our presence. Perhaps it's the novelty of having us show up unannounced that gives her the ability to be in the moment, unfazed by Tanya's disappearance. As it turns out, Emma hadn't seen Tanya for over a week. Maybe by now, she's come to a place of temporary acceptance, the place a lot of kids have to get to in order to survive terrifying circumstances that are beyond their control.

We leave the next morning, Kay and Don grateful to us and heartbroken to see Emma go with us; they had been carrying the same dream of Tanya, Sam, and Emma, the one where they miraculously pull off a life together, living near them.

Emma is the perfect traveling child. She doesn't cry,

whine, fuss—all the while playing quietly with the toys Gemma packed in a kit bag for her. Other passengers, most of whom sit near us, make approving comments filled with praise about Emma's behavior.

"I wish all kids would behave as well as she does."

"Where did you get her? Heaven?"

"Can you train our kids to behave the same way as she does? We'll pay."

I want to tell these people that it has nothing to do with us. Emma is a wise child who has already figured out what she needs to do to survive and help the adults around her survive as well. I want to tell them that Emma has been deeply loved by her mother, cherished, adored, and honored by her, but also abandoned by her. I want to tell them that somewhere inside of Emma, she knows that this trip to Vermont with Gemma and me is just the beginning of the long, but anticipated separation from her mom, who, up until now, has been the greatest love of her young life.

Tanya and Emma run toward each other in, what appears to be, slow motion. I watch as they touch for the first time in months. It looks as if they will devour one another with voracious intensity. All of their senses seem to be raging, open and entirely engaged in the process of taking in as much of each other as conceivable. It actually looks painful to me, like they might be hurting each other.

I wonder what it must be like to love your mother with such ferocity. I did not know that kind of love with my own

mother, ever. She was not capable of that sort of selfless adoration for her children, her stark Christian upbringing ripping
that potential right out of her chest. Having five daughters in
close succession did not help, so by the time I was eight and a
half, our mother was spent, choosing to leave us to be raised
by our father. It was a survival tactic; we are all sure that if she
had not moved out of the house, her mental collapse would
have taken a particularly dark turn and maybe taken one or
more of us with her.

When I watch Emma and Tanya embrace upon first meetings, it always reminds me of a scene from the movie, *The Miracle Worker*, the story of the early life of Helen Keller and her
teacher, Annie Sullivan. Helen (played by Patty Duke) has
been taken to a small cottage by Annie Sullivan (Anne Ban-
croft), who insists that the only way Helen will finally come to
trust her, is if they are alone together, without the constant
interference of Helen's overly protective parents. After the
agreed upon time is up, a couple of weeks later, the mother appears, ready to take Helen back. Helen senses her mother's
presence immediately, when she smells her perfume in the
room. The resulting embrace is volcanic, mother and daughter gripping each other for dear life. Their love seems almost
too raw for the watchful eyes of others. That is how I have always viewed the embraces of Tanya and Emma. Am I envi-
ous? I'm not sure but watching them now, my impulse is to get
away from them as quickly as I can. Whatever kind of love this
is, I cannot be near it. And whatever kind of love this is, it cannot sustain Tanya's grip on her three-month-old sobriety.

I am walking back into the house after taking Basia out for her morning constitutional. I had to kick a lot of snow off of my boots; there was a sizeable storm during the night and all is quiet outside now.

From the mudroom, I can hear Gemma wailing, "NO. NO!" I immediately imagine the two maimed bodies of Emma and Tanya—a car wreck; knife wounds; charred and burned flesh beyond recognition.

I rush to her side. "What happened? Gemma, what is it?"

She points to the phone machine. The phone machine? I am completely confused.

"Emma called and left two messages last night. We didn't hear them. I didn't hear the phone."

I listen then. At first I can't understand what Emma is saying—she doesn't sound right. Her voice is guttural, animal, a wounded animal.

"Gigi! Kiki! Momma's gone! Gigi! Kiki!"

Oh my fucking God.

"I'm alone! Momma's gone. Gigi! Kiki!" She screams our names over and over again—the sound of her five-year-old voice tearing every fiber in my body from its mooring on bone.

We didn't hear the phone ring!

I turn off the machine and reach for the receiver, dialing Tanya's number as fast as my fingers will move to the digits. Gemma grabs the receiver,

"Tanya? You're home? Where the fuck were you last night?" Her eyes have gone purple.

"Out getting milk? In a snowstorm? Of course you got stuck, you fucking asshole! What is wrong with you?"

"She's all right now? What did she do? Watched television till you got home? Yes she called us. We didn't hear it. Don't you dare give me any shit over this, Tanya. I'll fucking rip your head off, do you understand? Put Emma on, right now."

"Are you all right, honey? I'm so sorry, Emma. Kiki and I didn't hear the phone ring."

Guilt and shame do not return to places of rest without some kind of struggle. Gemma and I process our feelings for months afterward. Inside every cell, the image of Emma sitting alone in front of the television while a snowstorm raged just outside her reach lives on. The image may one day fade into shades of black and white and the colors that mark it with blood reds and nauseating browns and greens, will diminish into transparent washes. But a part of that image will remain imbedded within each of us, along with the sound of Emma's terrified voice, calling out our names, forever.

Within weeks of that phone message, left purposefully on our machine so we could play it for Tanya, something we never got to do, Emma came to us again, this time for good.

2
THE BIG BANG THEORY
OF FAMILY DYNAMICS

*T*here is a January day, past and tense, when a desperate and ultimately kind act of surrender changed our lives forever. For good or bad, Emma was handed over to Gemma and me, by Tanya, who had brought a now five-year-old Emma as far as she could take her without destroying her spirit. Emma came to us in winter—cold and fallow and white—the world was asleep and waiting for what the warmth of a waxing spring sun would soon bring: a big bang, a concentrated nucleus of energy which would explode, forming an entirely new family dynamic for us all.

Gemma and I were aware that Tanya wasn't doing well, but we weren't aware of the severity of the coming crash. Tanya's relationship with sobriety had always been tenuous. She has been struggling with drug addiction for nearly thirty years, since she was thirteen and began to self-medicate for problems that were later discovered to be related to bipolar disorder.

And so it was, on that January afternoon, that Emma became our responsibility, a responsibility that comes with the endless messes and, some say, timeless rewards and life-affirming opportunities. "Here. You have to take her. She's not safe with me," Tanya said to Gemma as she handed her over. Gemma kept her eyes focused on Emma without showing any signs of emotion while Emma held on with one hand, the other hand clutching a paper bag filled with clothes, a pillow, and a sheet. Emma did not move or turn around as her mother walked away. Tanya disappeared then, driving off into a three-day bender while Gemma and I soothed, fed, and protected Emma, at the same time trying not to get fired from our full-time jobs. Those first few days, Emma moved in and out of our reality and the one she had been living in with Tanya during the formative years of her young life. Shaking whatever fear and anxiety plagued her dreams was a nightly process; Gemma and I felt that we had no idea how to help her get through these episodes.

Emma is holding onto the sides of her mattress, her small fists gone sheet-rock white. Her skin matches the white of the sky—soon it will snow again in this Year-of-the-Snows. Emma doesn't see Gemma or me. The cold morning light lets us see her face clearly; her eyes are open and she is speaking coherently but not to either one of us. She is speaking to someone beyond our realm of vision.

"No! Not this time! No!" she says over and over.

"We shouldn't wake her," I whisper, remembering someone's seemingly solid advice about people having nightmares and to not awaken them because it would scare the wits out of them — rendering them insane.

"What are we supposed to do?" Gemma asks.

"Just hold her, I guess. I don't know," I say.

Gemma touches Emma's shoulder lightly. Emma pulls away as if she's been poked with a burning stick. Gemma continues to touch her even though neither one of us knows if that's the right thing to do.

A door, opened somewhere inside Emma, is letting in this terror, a terror so vivid it blocks out the light of day and anyone who might be there to offer help. We are not visible to her. The terror won't allow us to be seen.

I tell myself that these kinds of horrors in the night will only take place for a little while. These moments are finite. The day will come when Emma will return to her life with Tanya and then all of us will have our lives back. These moments are suspended animation, held in a murky wash, molecules in some colloidal soup. The elements will drop out of solution and carry on as always. This is temporary.

Emma's little mattress, tucked beneath the eaves of our bedroom, has already become cluttered with her possessions: a special Donald Duck and Mickey Mouse sheet complete with two burn holes; a small stuffed elephant and a bear; a tiny pillow named "Baby;" and a blanket. This nest has the look of permanence.

Emma finally wakes up. It isn't an instant snapping out of it. She begins to see us slowly, like we are coming to her from out of a thick mist. Soon she is reaching for Gemma, then clinging to her, saying she had a bad dream about the robber guy, a man who comes to rob her away from her momma.

"Oh, God," I think to myself. "She is already having nightmares about being stolen from Tanya and I'll bet Gemma and I are the robbers."

We haven't heard from Tanya yet. Gemma is convinced she's out using. Of course that's what she's doing. Why else would she disappear and not contact us? It's the same old pattern. But damn her if she thinks she can keep doing this: leave Emma when she wants to go on a binge, return, insist she is going to change this time, reclaim Emma, and then set off into a life that has no clear dimensions, understandable parameters, or promises of safety for Emma. But hold on. Isn't that exactly what I want? For all of our lives to go back to normal?

Tanya calls two days later. She has signed herself into a treatment center on the opposite side of Vermont. Can we keep Emma just a little longer? Just twenty-eight days longer?

The muscles are tightening in my jaw. I'm chewing my lips and nails. I pump around in bed at night as Gemma crawls down and over to comfort Emma. I try to find Gemma in that bed of ours but I can't. She's not there anymore.

We go to see Tanya. The drive takes over an hour and by the time we get there, I'm ready to scratch glass with my bitten nails. Instead, I walk quickly to the top of a hill while Gemma and Emma visit with Tanya. I pass three trailers on my way up the hill. Squalid and desolate, these places only serve to agitate me even more, because they make me think of desperate, uneducated people who are leading inconsequential lives, somewhat like the life Tanya is currently living. I walk faster and faster until I run out of breath, stopping by the side of the road to bend over, with pain rising into my chest and lower abdomen. I almost vomit from the throbbing blood, which has given my throat a strong taste of iron. I look down into a ditch running along the asphalt. A wet, old newspaper is oozing down the road, coming apart as it pulls away from the glue of the print. The slimy mass looks like an inner organ, gone soft and ready for the final moments of dissipation. I reach down to touch this newspaper glop, hoping to find some words of comfort or wisdom. The pages have been wiped away of any discernible writing and so I am left standing with shredding sheets of wet newspaper in my hands, falling away like the skin from a badly sunburned back. I continue to stare as the large pieces disintegrate, hitting the pavement and then instantly turning into a translucent, jelly-like substance that rolls off in all directions, disappearing into the shadows of the ditch.

No words from the wise tucked between the folds of some forgotten newspaper. No words for me to carry back are able to convey to Gemma, Tanya, and Emma without having to speak.

Gemma, Emma, and Tanya are still visiting in the kitchen, a long, narrow room painted egg-yolk yellow—a yellow that has begun to fade into war-torn yellow. I am sure these walls have seen life in all its forms of spit, snot, tears, vomit, and blood. Have these walls also seen the kinder side of human behavior? I want to believe it but I can't. I won't. I've been in the rooms of Alcoholic Anonymous. I have seen what goes on—the myopic focus leading to the selfish tirades, the little lives cracked open for all to witness, the slide into self-delusion in order to feel better about the messes they have made. Don't get me wrong. I believe that A.A. has saved lives and that, in fact, it saved mine. But I'm mad right now. Madder than any fucking hatter could possibly be and even the brilliance of A.A. is lost on me right now. Maybe if I look a little closer.

Perhaps there have been caring meals served here— prayers of thanks given. Maybe voices were raised in song, blessings on the food and the day. Maybe, for a little while, the rage was set aside and the walls held their color as the sun blazed and bounced the gatherers' slim feelings of hope throughout the room. And then, maybe those feelings of hope became so large and powerful that they busted out into a day that was ready to accept them and send them higher, maybe even a little further on. Maybe the feelings became voices that were lifted up toward the light of the sun as it illuminated those yellow walls with glimmers of some kind of forgiveness that could be felt by all of us.

I stand back and look a little closer at the trio before me. The rectangular tables, those brown things that every institution owns and uses until they have become threadbare, practically becoming paper, hold small clusters of mealtime fare: octagonal salt and pepper shakers, white paper napkins, small pea-green vases, pink sugar packets, and clear glass ashtrays. The tables are worn down in spots from heavily burdened elbows and heavily heaped plates.

I wait and watch. All this waiting allows for these observations of place. I resent it, this waiting. As I wait, the walls begin to creep in toward me. Everything is becoming square and squared off. There are lots of corners. These are close quarters. Tight quarters. No space left. No space right. A quadrilateral. A box. A FUCKING BOX. They come at me from all corners of the room. This tribe of Sicilians that Gemma, Emma, and Tanya belong to. They want my blood. They extract the essentials, shed their skin, and move on.

The walls have just about closed in as far as they can go when I am stopped by the expression on Tanya's face. She looks completely at odds with her own face. Undone. Maybe she has never been done. Maybe she was never given what all children need in order to form their outer cloaks, the ones that protect them from dark harm. Tanya doesn't seem to be wearing such a cloak. She is not properly dressed for this world and, thus exposed, must feel the winter and all cold things that strike without warning.

I wave goodbye to her without being able to find any kindness. My hand flutters up and back down with no affection. If I had to touch her now, my upper lip would curl up in disgust. I'm sure her skin is scaly and unprotected and I will never touch her again as long as I live. I swear.

Then I see Emma get up, hug her mother and turn toward me. How can she touch Tanya? Perhaps it is because she is a child and doesn't sense the dangers yet. Perhaps it is because Tanya is her mother. All children become familiar with sensory insults that come with loving their parents. Emma has become familiar with scales and dark and no cloak and she can seemingly walk away unscathed. But maybe not.

Gemma and I will take Emma out of here. We will erase the brown tables and dark corners and scaly skin from her consciousness. We will give her new skin to touch. We will teach her how to put on a cloak. I promise.

As we walk away from the rehab center, Emma walks extremely close to me. I pull her even closer until her face is pressed against my right thigh. There is no struggle, no turning around and yelling for her mother. Emma comes with Gemma and me as if she has always been coming with us, as if the script was written a long time ago. Once safely strapped into the car seat right behind my side of the car, Emma begins to cry quietly, trying hard not to alert us to her feelings; she stuffs her face into the little pillow that she carries everywhere. Gemma and I exchange looks of the broken-hearted. What can we do for Emma as we drive away from this place of shredded dreams?

That night Emma dreams of the robber again. It is a particularly violent episode, almost a seizure. The dream grips her and holds on. She sits on her mattress and screams for over an hour, her body rigid and her eyes staring. Gemma lies with her until the dream recedes. Twisting in bed, listening through the feathers of my down pillow to Emma's muffled screams and Gemma's even more muffled whispers, I take the promises I made earlier to Emma and toss them to the darkness. "Let Emma find her own new skin. I didn't ask for this. I don't want this." Barely relieved, I eventually fall into the kind of sleep that can only be described as tortured.

I wake up after about four hours of sleep, looking for someone to blame for all this. When Gemma tries to roll in for a morning hug, I roll away wordlessly and get out of bed. I don't ask her if she would like a cup of tea, something I've been asking her every morning these last six years or so, ever since the ritual began inadvertently.

Once in the kitchen, I make Gemma her cup of Earl Grey tea anyway. Not making it would be too dangerous, too risky, too close to some kind of admission of impending relationship doom. Gemma comes downstairs and walks directly into my arms, where I receive her gladly. I hate starting the day angry with her and I can't do it now.

"I know this is hard for you, my love. What can I do for you?" she asks with the tenderest sincerity, her sage-green eyes soft and responsive.

I'm about to tell her what she can do for me. The words are

forming, taking shape and moving forward and down into my mouth.

"You can pay a little more attention to me. You can make love with me. You can cut me a little slack," is what I would have said if given the chance.

But then, from upstairs, Emma calls out, "Where are you, Gigi?" using the name she gave Gemma when she was two years old.

"Right here, sweetie!" Gemma replies instantly, touching my face lightly as she turns and hurries upstairs to Emma.

I look down at our dog, Basia. She has been listening to everything and waiting patiently for someone (me; I have been and now even more so, the one who walks the dog) to take her outside and across the street to the small patch of woods next to the hospital where she poops in the morning.

"It's you and me, Twirly." I stroke her head, using one of her nicknames.

I layer myself up: vest, parka, hat, mittens, boots, snow pants, wool socks. I realize that I am dressing for a long winter's journey and not just a short walk across the street with my dog, Basia, so she can do her morning ablutions.

By the time I close the front door behind me I am angry at Gemma again. What's worse is that I am also angry at Emma for being the cause of my anger toward Gemma, and that scares me.

We have moved Emma's mattress, sheets, "baby," and stuffed animals into the guest room. Under the eaves of the bedroom next to ours, we start to establish a space for Emma that is hers, away from us. She can still come and sleep with us or have one of us sleep with her, but from now on, she has her own room.

Gemma decides to go up to Tanya and Emma's apartment, empty the place out, and retrieve any personal belongings that Emma might be attached to, in order to help Emma with this, the latest of transitions. Gemma brings a couple of friends with her, while I tend to Emma.

The three women enter. Through the hallway, long and narrow, the small windows don't allow in much light. The thick, black-painted door stands locked. Gemma wields the key and enters first. She holds still as she views the remains of a life promised. She shuts the door for a moment before she lets the others in. Gemma is afraid of what she will find. But this is not the time to hesitate. Tanya is gone. Emma needs clothes, toys, and books. Gemma opens the door and the women begin to go through the apartment.

At first, the sorting seems easy. Bits of paper, food, and clothes seem normal enough. But then, the door to the back room is opened. No one is expecting this:

Mountains. Heaps. Cigarettes. Socks. Bottles. Dolls. Pillows. Glasses. Food. Cardboard. Glass. Wood. Magazines. DVDs. Letters. Stuffed Animals.

It is all here. In thousands of frenzied moments, this room became the place where everything was tossed. When the phone rang and Gemma said she was coming over, this is where the cigarettes were thrown. This is where the socks, filled with pieces of last night's dinner, ended up. This is where the dream ended.

In the back room of an apartment in Putney, Vermont, a good-bye was acknowledged. A good-bye to a dream held by so many of us: a dream of a life realized for Tanya and Emma. A golden dream that no longer had any chance of coming true.

3

I Didn't Want One

I wanted a child of my own for about two weeks back when
I was thirty-seven. Was it my biological clock? Societal
expectations? It was probably both of those things. The urge
was short-lived, what with Gemma's adamant resistance (she
insisted we would be terrible at raising a child together. That's
come to bite us both in the relationship ass). And with a voice
of reason vehemently screaming at me, I knew enough to let
it go. And very glad of our final decision we were.

With great relief, Gemma and I continued to enjoy life
without the demands of motherhood. Gemma and I even
gloated at times. We looked out at those with children and
gloried in our unencumbered existence. We had only a dog to
care for, thank goodness, and even that was a challenge sometimes.

There is a delicious satisfaction in being able to turn children back over to their parents when those children have become unruly or when their sweet voices have become grating, when cute has dissolved into obnoxious or when the limits of patience have been reached. "Here, you take her back now." Those are the saving words, words that as a teacher, aunt, or grandparent you are allowed to utter without flinching or feeling any guilt.

There is no turning Emma over anymore. There is no "Tanya, come and get her." Not now. Now there is: "It's your turn to put her to sleep." "I'll get up, it's OK." "Can you please do it?" "Would you really mind?" "I'm so tired."

This kind of turning over is still new to me; I'm not sure I'll ever get used to it. Yes, I care about Emma and yes, I hold her close to me and feel my heart loosen and then beat out a rhythm of acceptance. But how can I know the deeper love of the blood bond? Of the aching love that comes from inside the cells? That doesn't mind the "Here, you take her?" How can I know the love that sings beyond all reason, beyond time and imagination? I can't and so, even in my desire to love Emma, in my evolving surrender, there are still elusive distances, layers of breath that keeps us separate. She doesn't belong to me and I don't want her to.

During the impossible moments it doesn't much matter whom she really belongs to. The strain of trying to behave admirably has wrapped around my neck muscles like Theraband strips and I am rendered paralyzed with a sense of defeat.

Last night, I pushed Emma. In front of Gemma and Debbie, a friend of Emma's who was spending the night; I pushed her hard enough to send her across the bedroom toward her mattress, the place I was originally intending her to go. Defiant and angry, Emma had stood in front of me, her face a fuming mask of direct rage. "You read this book to me, or else!" she screamed.

"No," I answered, calmly as a coiled viper.

Emma dug her dirty little feet into the maple floor, her arms crossed, refusing to budge. Debbie and Gemma watched as Emma and I squared off. "God, I hate this. I hate this testing. This wouldn't be happening if she wasn't here," I was thinking to myself with a growing sense of panic. I was losing control. Then, with one more look at Emma's aggressive expression, I lost control and I pushed her. Through the calm and into the panic. Right through the reason. Right through the feigned nice. I pushed her.

Emma, of course, began to wail. Gemma swooped in for the rescue, picking her up and taking her into our bedroom, leaving me lying with a puzzled-looking Debbie. Without a word of protest, she lay down next to me on the mattress that was positioned next to Emma's. I began to read the book she had chosen before Emma had so rudely insisted that they read the book she wanted to read. Debbie remained lying there like a small beached whale, unable or afraid to move.

Emma eventually returned and took up next to my free left side. I apologized for pushing her, saying, "I really got angry when you stood in front of me that way. I wish we could've solved the problem another way."

"OK, OK. Let's read," she said. I didn't insist on an apology.

I thought that Gemma was going to let me have it, the punishing lecture later that evening, after the girls were asleep. She didn't.

"Hard moment, huh? She was jealous of Debbie. She thinks we're treating her nicer. Are we?"

"Aren't you supposed to treat guests with some measure of respect?" I asked with a defensive tone.

"Yeah, but c'mon. Emma doesn't understand that. She's only six," Gemma wisely stated.

"Aren't we supposed to be teaching her these things?" I asked.

"Not now, honey. Yes. Yes. Just not now. I'm going up to check in on them. I'll be right back."

As I lie on the couch watching *Queer Eye for the Straight Guy* ("This place screams women's correctional facility!" yells Carson), phrases like "Pick your battles," "Don't sweat the small stuff," and "Easy does it" keep filtering through my mind, phrases that are common utterances in Alcoholics Anonymous meetings. Can I please have one night when I am not in conflict with myself over my lousy behavior? *Queer Eye for the Straight Guy* almost does the trick. I almost escape. When Gemma returns, we don't talk about Emma or anything related to her. We might both be hovering around admonishments and blames and ultimate forgiveness, but for now we sink into the mindless and, somehow, kind prattle of the Fab Five.

The snows have come again. Just when we thought this re-
prieve would last as least into the weekend, another blizzard
moves up the East Coast. It's a rouser, a storm that gets me up
off the couch to take periodic peeks at its form and style. This
one has gusts of wind that slam in sideways—the streetlights
outside our house lending an orange tint to the large flakes as
they fly in from the northeast. The storm also compels me to
get up and watch the Weather Channel—the green precipitation blob that oozes across the screen has always been a
source of fascination. I sit mesmerized, content and elated as
the storm builds—the green growing darker and darker, indi-
cating a more potent, thicker, and richer storm. I always want
the green to go deeper, to bury itself in orange and then
change to red—then we would really be in a doozy.

This particular storm is not one of those, although it is de-
cent. As I am watching the green blob of precipitation, Emma
sleeps upstairs, dreaming beneath it, and Gemma is also beneath
it, reading silently. Tanya is beneath it, too, trying desperately to
score. She is not successful and winds up getting arrested.

"Jesus Christ!" I blurt out when Gemma tells me what has
happened the next day. "What is wrong with her?" As if I
didn't know.

Gemma looks at me with what seems to be an expression
of contempt and it sets me off.

"What? I can't express myself? I can't respond to the stu-
pidity of your sister's insane impulses?" Then she glares and
points upstairs. Of course, Emma is directly above us. Nothing can be expressed openly now. Nothing.

"Don't you think I would like to scream and shout about this, too? I could use your support right now," Gemma whispers through exasperation and frustration—the tightest lips on her.

"I don't know how to do this, Gemma."

"You don't want to do this, Carol."

"For God's sake. What do you expect?"

"A grown-up."

Fuck you. Fuck you. Fuck you. Over and up, back and down, around, crashing right through this one again. No reason why it shouldn't come up right now without anywhere to go with it.

"Goddamn you. Goddamn you!" I turn away from her. I want to go out into what's left of the storm, let it take what is left of me. But I don't. I turn back and face her.

"It's a good thing you turned around," she says. It doesn't exactly feel like a thank you to me, which is what I want her to say.

"This is not fair, Gemma."

"I know it is not fair. You, of all people, should know just how not fair life is. You'd better decide if this is something you can do with me because if you can't . . ." Gemma doesn't finish.

"What? You'll leave with Emma? I don't think so."

Gemma doesn't answer but continues looking at me with a less convincing glare.

"She just barely arrived. I'm not used to it."

"I hate to tell you, as if you didn't already know this, but

Emma is going to be with us for a long time." Her eyes do not leave mine.

"I need to go out," I say quietly.

"Can you take Emma outside to play so I can make a few phone calls?"

Didn't she hear what I said? If I don't take Emma out, Gemma will explode into me. If I do take her out, there is the chance that I will explode into Emma. I choose the former.

"I need to go out alone for a little while. Then I will take her out." I'm hoping that our relationship will survive this particular turning away, that Gemma will come back to understanding what I am going through before I come back in from the cold.

The awful behaviors that I have been exhibiting lately rise up from subterranean tunnels—they support my contention that I should not have a child to help raise. The unresolved issues that I thought were lying beneath in the caverns of finished business still exist, and Emma's presence has given them an excuse to rise again. The issues push up against the behavioral roots like underwater river rats or crazed moles. In those moments I am uncontrollable and unrestrainable. I can't stop what happens as the behaviors twist and grow toward the light of Emma's existence in my life. She is the light that these behaviors are drawn to, fed by the energy of the ancient pains and confusions of the past. It's baffling. It's beyond the reach of therapy, or, at least, any therapy I am aware of. Or maybe therapy is not what is called for here. I didn't want a child and I still don't. I don't want this one. How do I therapize that?

When not engaged in my own form of self-examination, I find myself watching other people who have children. I want to know how they behave toward their kids. Maybe in this watching I will find clues about how to want a child.

I watch when they don't know that I'm watching. Since I am a teacher, and have perfected the art of clandestine observation, it is easy to put on all kinds of facial expressions that convey interest and understanding as I search for signs. There are many expressions and postures that seem familiar and I think, "Yes, I've felt that, too." The exasperation when the kid doesn't comply. The adoration and relief when she behaves just as you had hoped she would. The terror when you believe she is hurt beyond your knowledge of the injury.

Then there are expressions and postures that I don't recognize and I think, "Now there's an expression of pure wanting if I've ever seen one." The look is usually drippy, as if the parent is about to cry with the most intense feeling of adoring ebullience. These looks resemble states of rapture that a religious zealot, having a direct communication with some kind of Holy Spirit, must look like. But since I've only seen that seeming state of rapture portrayed in the movies (for example; in the movie *Hawaii*, when Max von Sydow's character is praying for the pagan souls of the natives and he gets all rapturous as he communes with what he believes to be God), I am not entirely sure. That is not a whole lot to go on for recognizing states of rapture as they relate to wanting a child. So I think that if these are signs, I'm not convinced. I decide to come right out and ask some parents.

"Why did you want to have children?"

Not surprisingly, the answers do not stray from within a narrow band of responses. I expected most people to answer that they had to have children as if it were a life plan, a destined path, a primal course set by biology and perhaps by a god (Max von Sydow's, perhaps). And, for the most part, that is the answer.

I don't question that answer. I don't begin an argument with the phrase, "That's a load of bunk." Who is to say what we are destined for? What our bodies demand of us? If there is a God or not?

The people who respond with, "Well, we didn't want one, exactly. We (got to love the "we") got pregnant and decided to have the baby," look at me like I'm seriously defective when I ask, what is to me, the most important question of all: "How did you come to want the baby after it was born?" I don't think my question is stupid. It gets to the fundamental heart of it. How do we get to want something we didn't want in the first place, especially if that something is a child? The parents who give birth or adopt (after years of planning) have time to get ready for the wanting. Their bodies and minds prepare for it. The arrival of a child then brings out the final wanting and the process is complete. It takes time, imagining, hope, and belief to want a child. It takes a certain view of the future.

My friend Elaine married a man with two young children and then, a few years later, had a child of her own with her husband. Although she adores the stepchildren, she admits that she will never love them the way she loves her own son.

When I hear this, I feel closer to the kind of truth I have been looking for. I grab at her for more information. I pound at her to set me straight, to give me guidance, to set me on a course toward wanting and, finally, loving Emma. She tells me that I should not try and make anything happen, that I should let my relationships with Emma and Gemma unfold naturally. Give it some time, maybe three years or so. THREE YEARS? She isn't even going to be with us for three years. Isn't there some kind of condensed version for being trained to want someone or something that you didn't want?

"I was searching and hoping to find something more," I say, "a clue about wanting."

"Wanting has got nothing to do with it," Elaine wisely responds.

I think, *What if I never get to a place of really wanting Emma? It sounds so vile and rude and immature. But what if I never want her in the way that parents (biological or adopted) do? What if this limbo-like, half-state of wanting is the best I can do?*

It just has to be enough. Doesn't it?

4

An Electric Storm Named Tanya

I first met Tanya in the summer of 1994 on a trip Gemma and I had finally agreed to take after much debate. I had already heard too many sad and disturbing stories about her from Gemma; my reluctance to come face-to-face with her was undeniably obvious. But as the length of our relationship grew, so did the transparency of my excuses to avoid meeting Tanya. The time had arrived.

Gemma and I drove three hours to a coastal town in Massachusetts and waited for Tanya in the parking lot next to an International House of Pancakes. Gemma and I stood next to her gray Honda Civic, fidgeting with our hands and arm jewelry, of which she had more than I did. Gemma was wearing three bracelets on either arm, three rings, and some kind of leather band with shells sewn into it; I guess you could call that a bracelet, too. I was wearing two rings and a wristwatch that I had inherited from my sister, Danielle, who had died from leukemia the year previous. It was a scuba diving watch and although I had never scuba dived, I wore it to stay connected to Danielle. Since this watch had recently been fastened to her skin, there might even be a few cells mashed into the back face of it, cells that would rub off onto my skin. And every time I looked at it, I thought of Danielle, weightless and free, beneath the surface of the South Pacific Ocean. She had been to Pago Pago in 1991, clerking for a judge as she waited for the results of the bar exams.

It was Danielle I was thinking about as a red convertible sports car streaked into the parking lot. Pulling up next to Gemma's car, the sports car stopped within an inch of a chain-link fence that separated the IHOP parking lot from another parking lot just like it.

"Hey, girls!" shouted a woman from behind the wheel of the car.

"Tanya!" responded Gemma in a voice I had never heard her use before: clear, shrill, and concerned.

As they embraced, I had time to look Tanya over. There she was at last, the infamous one: Tanya of Gemma's Nightmares.

Then, she turned to look at me. If I could have, I would have looked away but I knew that would be rude, so I forced myself to stay facing her. The gaunt face, eyes, and lips accented by black and red makeup, was flickering at me with the speed and intensity of a strobe light. I was instantly disoriented. Each of Tanya's features seemed to be moving all on its own, as if some coherent and conscious force was dictating each nerve and muscle. They were plugged into their own electrical circuits, each one connected to a different animating source. Cheeks were bulging, lips were pursing, eyes were roving, and nostrils were flaring. And her hair: spitting copper-wire bundles frizzing off toward the four directions of heaven. Tanya was plugged into her own high voltage lines. The cocaine she snorted must have been from cocoa plants that were grown on live volcanoes in the mountains of South America.

I was afraid to hug her, afraid that I would get high just from the skin contact. But I hugged her anyway, with my eyes closed, my breath held in, and every muscle tensed.

"You look just like I thought you would," said Tanya. "You got great taste, Sis." She winked at me. "Let's eat."

Tanya lit a cigarette on our way into the restaurant. She had just enough time to take two quick inhalations before we reached the entrance and threw the lit cigarette on the top cement step, without putting it out. She opened the door like it was her own front door and walked in.

During the course of our meal, Tanya talked primarily about home-improvement ideas. ("We're buying a new living room set. The new one will really go good with the wood paneling.") Tanya left the table four times, twice to make phone calls and twice to use the bathroom. Her order of a rare cheeseburger, French fries, onion rings, and a salad remained untouched on the platter. She didn't even pretend to eat. She drank three Cokes and two glasses of water. When Gemma and I were nearing the end of our Caesar salads, Tanya said,

"I'm going outside for a cigarette." She threw a fifty-dollar bill onto the table. "It's my treat. Meet ya outside." She vanished as quickly as a handful of powdered sugar that has been tossed into a class-five hurricane.

"I don't think I can be around her, Gemma. Do we have to spend the night?"

"We already promised her we would. It's only for one night. Is it that bad?"

"Yuh-huh. And this is typical?" I already knew the answer.

"This is Tanya, my baby sister, since she was thirteen."

I looked at my watch. I would've taken Danielle, sick and dying, over Tanya, addicted and living, any day. The only problem was that Danielle was already dead and Tanya was not.

I had no choice but to accept Tanya and create some kind of relationship that would be cordial, maybe even amusing at times. But I was convinced that I would never come to love her, not even for Gemma's sake. When Tanya broke the news to us that she was pregnant and was going to keep the baby, my only thought was, "Oh great. Now she is going to destroy a child's life along with her own. How fair is that?"

Emma has been coming toward us for a long time, maybe since the moment of her conception. Funny how even when you know something, or someone, is on its way, you can deny its approach until the very last moment, right before it hits. Believe me when I say that I was not consciously aware that Emma was heading in our direction until that January afternoon when Tanya left her with us, for, what turned out to be, a very long winter's night.

5
RISE AND FINE

Gemma and I are being watched. Emma is sitting up on her mattress, blankets off and scattered on the floor; she is watching us. Her dark hair is a mess of beaten tangles as if she's been mashing her head all over everything, all night. She sits silently, which is unusual. Most mornings she either has to be awakened forcefully by one of us in order to get up for school or she crawls into bed with us within seconds of opening her eyes.

The heat of her eyes is invading, steady in its focus. I can't believe that Gemma has not felt it yet and I am tempted to kick her awake so she will deal with it. If I am the one to rise, then Emma will just have to take her chances with me and whatever mood comes with this rise and shine. Each day is different and I can barely keep up with my own vacillating morning moods.

Emma still isn't talking or moving and I am beginning to wonder if she's feeling all right. I poke my head up over our covers and look at Emma sitting there, bare legs spread onto the floor, her arms wrapped around her "Baby," the little pillow that accompanies her everywhere except school. She isn't even on the mattress. What is she doing? She puts a finger to her mouth to keep me quiet so Gemma can continue sleeping. I nod my head and sneak out from under the quilt. Gemma sleeps on—our movements and sounds have not gotten through to the world of dreams she inhabits. Emma has already crossed the room and takes my hand for the stairs descent, before I can even stop for a bathroom break. Basia is up now, too, ready for her routine to begin.

"Basia needs to go out, Kiki," Emma states, using the nickname she now calls me and has called me since she was about two.

"Looks like you'll have to come with us," I state back.

"It's too cold, Kiki," she protests.

"I'll bundle you up."

"Can't I just play quietly until you come back?"

She's got a point. But what if I take longer than planned?

"Then you have to promise to wake Gemma right away if you need anything important. But try and wait if it's not important. OK?"

"I promise."

She immediately moves toward the TV but before she can turn it on, I stop her.

"No television," I instruct.

"Awwwwwww. Why not?" she whines.

"It's too early and it might wake Gemma."

"I'll listen to it real quiet," Emma says.

"No, Emma," I say emphatically.

"What can I do then?"

"Play? Go get some dolls or coloring stuff and play till I get back. I'll only be gone a couple of minutes. Go on."

Reluctantly, Emma heads upstairs while I get dressed to go outside in ten-degree weather, Basia watching every move I make.

"Are you watching me, too? All right, all right. Knock it off. I don't like being watched," I say to Basia.

Then I hear voices from upstairs. I walk over to the bottom of the stairs and listen.

"No. You can't watch TV. Did you wake me up just to ask me that, Emma? For God's sake, where's Carol?" Gemma is complaining.

I am putting my gloves on when they both come down the stairs. The gloves feel real tight, like I am wearing the wrong pair.

"Couldn't you have handled this, Carol?" Gemma is already in glaring mode.

"I did handle it. I told her she couldn't watch TV."

"Those are my gloves you are putting on. Don't wear those, OK? You'll stretch them out, "Gemma commands crossly.

I look at my hands. I don't understand how I could have

mistakenly put on Gemma's gloves. Hers are black, mine are purple.

"Those aren't your gloves, Kiki," Emma reiterates from behind Gemma.

"What? I need you to order me around, too?" I ask irritably.

"They're not yours. That's all I mean," Emma says.

"No kidding."

"Are you going to take them off?"

I don't answer her. Instead, I pry them off using my teeth and throw them, inside out and crumpled up, onto the living room rug. I grab my own gloves and stomp out the door.

I am outside again, walking Basia, in the wake of another round of morning tension. As usual, Basia looks at me as we begin our walk, trying to gauge my emotional condition. Long strides and violent kicks at the snow prompt her to walk behind me, looking more like a dirty, brutalized sheep than a proud, upstanding black Labrador retriever. Her ears have all the dignity of overcooked mushrooms lying withered on either side of her head. She has no tail; it is totally lost somewhere beneath her body. I stand and wait as she catches up to me, make her sit so I can look her right in the eyes and say, "It's all right, Twirly. Can you please stop the tortured look? It's hard enough. Please?"

Not convinced, she continues to sulk behind me. I ignore her as we reach the woods. It takes her what seems like half an hour to find the perfect place to go. I am doing my best to thwart all impulses to throw ice balls at her. I throw them at trees instead. My aim is good this morning as the small and large maples become covered with splattered balls of snow and ice. I create a ring of polka-dotted trees, whirling and throwing as fast as I can.

By the time Basia has finished her morning ablutions, the winds have picked up and a misty snow is falling. I begin rehearsing my "fine" lines, the ones that will help me get back into the house with some semblance of grace and without the chance of an argument with Gemma.

"I was just feeling my oats."

"Life is just like a jungle gym, Gemma, and we are the monkeys."

"I don't know what came over me, I tell ya."

"It's PMS. It's just gotta be."

"It's got to be the low pressure system, I tell ya."

"I lost me marbles."

By the time I reach the front door, I am laughing out loud. When I look at Basia, I laugh even harder. Her face, still drawn up in an expression of some concern, gives the impression that she has heard the fine lines and is trying to understand the relevance they bear on the usual sequence of really important morning events, like a walk and breakfast.

"It's OK, Twirly. Not to worry. You're still getting that breakfast."

I walk in to find Emma watching television, holding her "baby," and wrapped up in her Disney sheet. A sippy cup full of Ovaltine sits propped on the couch next to her, waiting to be sucked dry.

I avoid eye contact with her; it's not that we would have it anyway. Once Emma is in front of the television set, like most children, there is no point in trying to get her attention. I slip by and into the kitchen where Gemma is having her cup of tea and Basia is already eating. I was hoping a perfectly rendered cup of coffee would be waiting for me on the kitchen table, but it isn't. Gemma has no understanding of coffee brewing mastery and hasn't attempted to learn. I am on my own with my plastic drip-filter contraption that makes the strongest coffee possible without becoming coffee stew.

Gemma looks up at me with a smile, an attempt at either an apology or neutrality. Instantly, I can sense that a "fine line" will not be necessary; we can bypass the morning script of the confused and the weary and go straight to the, "How are you, really?"

"I'm already exhausted," she says.

"Not good," I reply.

"No. I don't know how I'm going to make it through today. I hate plugging her into the TV. first thing but sometimes I just have to," she confesses.

"No one is watching or judging you, well, except for me. And I'll try not to, OK? It's a weekend. Let's try to give each other a break," I reply.

"So what's the plan, darling?" she asks.

"Oh, yeah. That," I say.

Without a plan, Gemma's normally intense and direct energy becomes diffuse and therefore, according to her, useless. Even before Tanya delivered Emma into our lives, Gemma had to have a plan for each and every day. With Emma on board the plan train, Gemma's need for a daily plan has increased proportionately to the kind of chaos a six-year-old child can create. I am just getting to the point now where I understand that she is not intentionally torturing me by insisting on a plan every morning. Gemma has to have a plan in order to function. It's that simple. I run a wild course each day within the confines of a sketchy plan or schedule. Obviously, neither approach is right or wrong, but we continue to fight over this issue passionately, arguing the benefits of the other's perspective with self-righteous devotion.

"Would you just try using a calendar or checklist, Carol? You wouldn't always forget appointments and things you need to get done. You can't keep everything in your head, especially at your age (nearing fifty)," Gemma says.

"C'mon, Gemma. You're so anxious all the time. Forget your lists for just one day and see how it feels. It could relax you for once," I say.

I want no part of a plan today. I want to ride out this one without periodic check-ins and chore-driven time tables. But before I can declare this a plan-free day, Gemma says, "I really need to do some grocery shopping and then I was hoping to go see Tanya. I've got to talk with her without Emma right there. We've got to make some plans. Is that all right with you?

I want to say, "You and Tanya can go fuck yourselves."

Instead, I say, "Well, yeah. I guess so. How long will you be?"

"A few hours. It won't take me that long since Tanya is closer now. Why? Did you need to do something?"

"I didn't have a plan, if that's what you mean."

"Can we not go there, please?"

"Go where?"

"Can we just deal with what needs to get done and not antagonize each other?"

Easy for her to ask, maybe even easy for her to do. I honestly don't know anymore since we hardly ever get a chance to try and understand each other these days. And so Gemma goes off into her well-planned day, leaving Emma and me to our day in the trenches of combined chaos.

Emma and I are making our way up a sledding hill, surveying our sledding options as we climb. The hill is close enough to our house to be able to walk to it but not while carrying two sleds, so we drove over. We didn't bring Basia, who does not seem to understand what sledding is, or, if she does, hates it with a canine fervor. Running alongside sled, toboggan, or disc, paying no attention to the obstacles that might cause her a good crash or tumble, Basia will try to bite the rider's legs, all the while barking feverishly. I have tried talking with her about it, even behaviorally trying to cure her of this need to bite happy sliders, but no form of intervention has ever worked. Basia cannot be cured of her loathing of sleds nor of her fear of toasters.

From the top of the hill, Emma and I can see straight up the Connecticut River Valley, northward. It has turned into a clear, cold day—a pinched wind making its way through the trees, right into our faces and down our necks. I stand quietly, made silent by the great beyond at our feet. The world's business goes on and on below us. Nothing of any consequence can reach us now—the hill, the air, the snow, the heights—there is no room for troubles.

"What are you looking at, Kiki?" Emma asks as she reaches me. It took her longer to walk up the hill than me so I've had a few moments to think.

"The valley. The mountains. The sky," I reply.

"Are we at the top of the world up here?" she wants to know.

"Pretty close to it. Can you see another place that could be higher than we are?" I ask.

"No. Not really," she replies.

"Then, I guess we are. Ready to go down?" I ask.

"Yep," she answers.

"Want to go alone or with me?" I ask, knowing she might not be ready for a solo run.

"With you first." That's what I thought.

We fit ourselves into the purple, plastic, oblong sled, Emma tucking herself securely between my formidable thighs. Planting my feet into the snow, I hold us back while we decide which route to take. There's the straight down run or the veer-off-to-the-right run; each has its clear advantage. Straight down is faster with not much of a flat stretch at the bottom on which to settle the nerves and body. The right run is longer and gentler with the kind of flat expanse that allows for plenty of wit gathering after the ride. I'm thinking we should take the right run for starters as our warm-up. But before I can push off, I ask Emma, "Which way?"

"That one," she says, pointing to the right run.

"Let 'er rip!" I yell and push us off.

Emma begins screaming as soon as we start moving. When snow starts flying into our faces, I start screaming, too. I use my gloved hands to steer us, keeping the sled headed onto the right track. Toward the bottom, our bodies leaning in different directions, the sled diverges from its path, turning into soft, loose snow, and we come to an abrupt stop, tumbling out of the sled and into the snow. Emma is laughing so hard, she gurgles, her saliva mixing with the snow that is covering her pink face. She rolls through the snow and over to me, climbing up onto my prone body. We are face to face. Her eyes are explosive blue, charged by the excitement of the ride. She is practically choking on snow and saliva mixture, inhalations and exhalations pulling the dripping mess back and forth— up into her mouth and back out again. Some of it falls onto me—right onto my lips. I sputter and wipe it away, laughing as I exclaim, "Hey! What's this? A fine thank-you for such a wild ride, I must say. The nerve. The very nerve."

Emma responds with a growling laugh, the source of which is so deep from inside her, it makes her body go completely limp in my arms. I continue with, "No more spit, I say. I won't have it. Off with ya."

I cannot roll her off of my body; she has become so heavy and stiff. Finally, I manage to get myself out from under her forty pounds and turn her over onto her back so she's facing the sky.

"Kiki!" She grabs my arm. "Wait. I can't breathe."

"Stop laughing, you goofball," I say, although she has already stopped laughing by this time. I start getting concerned when I see how serious she has suddenly become.

"I mean it, Kiki!" She is panting now.

"OK. Just calm yourself." I wipe the remaining snow and saliva mixture from her face and help her sit up. We sit quietly for a few minutes as she gets hold of her breathing, then she wipes her face on my sleeve, jumps up, and begins running toward the hill. Looking down at the mess she has left on my sleeve, I yell in response, "I am going to seriously get you for this!"

I reach her in three strides, pick her up from under her arms, and toss her over my back. Holding her by her boots, I hang her upside down as I trudge up the hill. After maybe ten steps, I bring her right side up, only to find that she is crying.

"What happened? Did I hurt you," I ask. I'm thinking that I've gone too far this time; somehow, I must've hurt her. She continues to cry and it feels that this is the beginning of a deluge, something larger is happening here. She can't be that badly hurt.

"What's the matter, Emma? It would really help me to know," I say gently.

A few more gulps and she spits it out, "I miss my momma!" She drags out the word "momma" so it sounds more like, "Ma ah mmmah ah ah ah." As she drawls out the very last "ah," her entire body droops away into suffocating sobs. I am barely able to hold her; it feels like there is nothing to put my arms around. I sit down in the snow, forming a little inlet for her to collapse into, and I let her cry. We stay this way for as long as

I can endure it. Creeping into my thoughts is a big word, a huge word followed by a huge forward motion. The word is, "NO!" and the motion is a screaming sprint away from Emma. These impressions rise without my permission. They set in without a sound on the most slippery of tiny feet. Here I am holding a crying child who has become abhorrent to me— whose very presence locks my heart up, thus denying her, or anyone else for that matter, access to me. I have fallen away into my resistance once more.

I continue to hold Emma while she cries out for her momma, the word "momma" now taking on the weight of a swear word banned by the authorities living inside of me who have no patience for little kids who cry out hysterically for their mothers. When my mother left my sisters and me when we were really young, I didn't cry like this. We had to be strong and Emma should just shut up and be strong, too.

I am cringing now, my shoulders inched up and forward. I force myself to take off a glove and touch Emma's face. Afraid that she might feel the aversion coming from my fingertips, I close my eyes and will some small stream of warmth to flow out from them. I drag around inside of me for anything resembling compassion and try to pass it on to my hands. Then I look at Emma's face; it has become really pink and wet, squeezed tight and wrinkled. She looks like a baby pig, a fetal pig, like the ones we dissected in anatomy and physiology class in college. She is soft against me now, her crying turning into a stilted breathing clogged with occasional gasps for air. There is no more crying for her momma. Whatever was conveyed in the touch of my hand, it has calmed her, or maybe she has calmed herself; the aversion that rose like poison into the upper reaches of my body has fallen back into storage sacs. I stroke her forehead with tenderness, pushing her hair back, away from her face.

"Are you OK, now?" I ask quietly.

She nods.

"Are you ready to go home?" I ask.

"No. I want to go down the hill again."

"Are you sure?"

"Yep." Her answer is loud and believable.

I wipe her face off as dry as I can get it with the back of my dry hand, kiss her on the top of her head, and help her up. We make our way up the hill together, holding hands.

Emma and I are sitting in the living room, drinking hot chocolate and watching the Nickelodeon Channel on television when Gemma gets home later that afternoon. She makes no eye contact with me as she walks past, going directly upstairs. From the top landing, she says, "Carol, we need to talk. Could you come upstairs?"

There is a splash of time to get ready for what Gemma is about to announce. I walk up the stairs with the best intentions in mind; I will be completely supportive of whatever it is she has to tell me. I will listen with all senses engaged, body turned directly toward her and my face open without any defenses barring her words. No arms folded across the chest in an armor stance. No javelins ridden up the derriere to force an exceptionally present moment when all my senses are yelling, "YAAAAAAHAHHHAHAHAHAHAHAH. We are listening and we are so listening big."

But then she tells me that Tanya is going to another reha-bilitation center, the name of which is Alice's Wonderland. This rehab is in Mesa, Arizona, which means that Tanya has to be gone for at least six months, maybe even longer, de-pending what the courts decide. Tanya wants Gemma and me to get legal custody of Emma so we can make medical, edu-cational, and therapeutic decisions for her without having to have Tanya sign off each and every time. I wish I could say that I did what I had intended to do, that I listened well, smiled bravely, and told Gemma that I would do anything to make this situation easier for her, for us. But I didn't.

By the time Gemma is finished, the poison has risen back up into my esophagus and I am just about gagging on it. I am trying desperately to think of something to say that will get me past my feelings of doom, rage, and powerlessness and that will make the vile liquid in my throat go down again. I am being pushed against the inside of a one-way tunnel. Water is on the way from a dam that has burst farther upstream. The only thing I have time for is to say my goodbyes and cast off into the coming floods.

"Carol. If you are about to tell me that you cannot do this or that Tanya is a fucked-up piece of shit or that you want our lives back or that you are feeling abandoned by me or whatever other selfish bullshit you look like you are about to say, you can forget it. I need you to either do this with me or I will do this by myself. I will not turn my back on Emma. I want you to do this with me, but if you can't then you have made your decision." She pauses to take a breath and turns directly to face me, in and close.

"I want to know what happened to the kind, generous, devoted, loving woman I married. Where is she?" She asks this last question as if she expects me to answer it.

6

HUMMINGBIRD

*G*emma and I go out for lunch and, to our surprise, Emma lets us; after eight months of staying home every day, it's about time. During our first attempt at getting away alone together about a month ago, Emma went straight for our throats with tear-enhanced sobbing, which quickly turned into high-pitched wailing unfit for human ears, and dog ears for that matter. Basia crept down into the basement to hide underneath the stairs for the duration of the tirade.

But once in the car this time, watching the curtains for any signs of a clawing hand trying to rip curtains, window, or babies (her stuffed pillow) to shreds, Gemma and I realize we have no idea where we are going and, truth be told, no real desire to go anywhere either. The exhaustion that so many parents have spoken about and we had so haughtily dismissed in the past is real, for God's sake. Now all I want to do is just sit here in the car, listening to absolutely nothing.

After a few minutes of listening to absolutely nothing, I want to cry. This can't be happening, this slide into parenthood without my permission. Or did I give permission inadvertently? Seems I can't remember anymore. Is being in a twelve-year committed relationship giving permission in itself? Does it go without saying? Am I supposed to be all soft and filled with new age love and acceptance? Is this another great "OPPORTUNITY?"

I imagine the face of a person that I ran into at the grocery store earlier in the day who looked at me with those glazed-over, blue-green eyes and said in a whisper filled with meaning and new age insight, "Having Emma come into your life is such an opportunity for you to deal with your own issues of abandonment." I smiled politely, but little did she know that I wanted to send her and everyone else who has uttered the word "opportunity" in the context of this situation, off to a prison camp for people who overuse the word "opportunity." At this camp, the only form of entertainment would be a nightly game of "Opportunity Knocks." The game would go something like this: each player would receive instructional cards that would force him or her to use the word "opportunity" in a story narrative or when trying to explain some deep new age razzmatazz and when a player uses the word (which would be inevitable and often, of course) then she or he would get "knocked" in the head with a baseball bat or branded with a branding iron leaving the word "OPPORTUNITY," burned

into a body part of their choosing. We, ignorant human be-
ings, normally leap for the one-liners, the clumped, saran-
wrapped witticisms that save us from really having to go the
extra mile with the poor soul who is desperately wanting some
guidance and keeps winding up at these shoddy gatherings
where people keep murmuring chant-like, "It's such an opportunity."

Gemma has never said to me, "This is such an opportunity for us." And it's a damn good thing, too. She has said other
things that have not exactly been to my liking, for instance,
the latest, "Where is the woman I married?" But somehow
nothing she has said ever seems as trite and condescending as
that lame excuse of a phrase, "This is an opportunity."

"Dinner?" she asks.

"A movie?" I ask.

"A walk?" she asks.

"Bowling?" I query.

"Making out?" she ventures.

I start the car hoping it will drive itself, and therefore us, to
a destination we hadn't thought of or maybe had thought of
but had forgotten. Because neither of us has enthusiastically
endorsed any choice yet, I turn the car toward the Marina, a
small restaurant by the mouth of the West River where it enters the placid Connecticut River. Even if we wind up having
nothing to say to one another, at least we will have the view.
It's not much of a view as views go and we have certainly seen
a few spectacular ones in our day, but for this particular spot
in southeastern Vermont, this view serves an extremely vital

purpose: it gives us perspective. It is our view toward distant ridges, which are out there beyond our short-sighted reality. The eyes need expansive views so they don't become focused solely on those things that are close by.

We have relatively short, dramatic sweeps here, not of the breadth and depth one might find in places with larger mountains like the Rockies or the Adirondacks. The drama here is about contrasts of line, color, and texture. It is the intensity of the deep green pine groves pushing up against a stand of birch far away to the west. It is the close-cropped hay field folding and undulating like a woman's back, soft, pink flesh bordered by the unwavering walls of old stone that run the lengths of fields and woods throughout Vermont.

Gemma and I sit and appreciate our dramatic sweep, the sun almost spent. I look at Gemma and ask myself if I've really loved her. Have I felt all pretenses, affects, and excuses roll away? I'm not totally convinced. Maybe it will take me a lifetime. Maybe loving Emma will teach me how to love Gemma better and deeper. Maybe by loving Emma, I will learn something I don't even know about love, not yet. I will not call this an opportunity; I will call it a chance or, better yet, a choice. Even if Emma winds up going back to Tanya in six months, it still makes sense for me to try loving Emma with sincerity and conviction.

Back home in the kitchen later that afternoon, Gemma and I are hugging, every hug an act of trying to move closer toward each other. Emma slips into the kitchen and inches in between us. The heat that just moments ago could clearly be felt by both Gemma and me, has had to be instantly squelched. We are now like three sea creatures, our arms extending as far as they will go, like tendrils. We touch through the three-way squeeze. I move one hand down to the top of Emma's head instead. I feel her hair, the brown strands moving in and out of my fingertips; I give her solace. I include her. I let her into this small circle. My intake of breath is short; it is holding back the life and love. I open my chest, and take in a deeper breath, a longer inhalation. I want to know the three of us for just a moment. I want to know what it feels like to have a child between us. I fear that I just don't know how. I want this to be real. When will my relationship with Gemma naturally take on another relationship? When will the gestation process be over? She is not my child. We didn't even have nine months to prepare for the incoming.

I look down at Emma. Her head is buried in Gemma's belly, both arms wrapped tightly around her middle. I continue to stroke Emma's hair; suddenly she looks up, our eyes meeting. What is she expecting? I'm not sure. A disapproving grimace? A surly frown? The looks of rejection and disdain which I have been trying to lose for the last several months?

Instead, I smile at her. I tell myself that this place is for the three of us now, if even for a short while. I smile again with my lungs full of breath, with my heart full of some kind of music. Emma smiles back. The doubtful expressions fall away and we are for an instant, simply the three of us, sharing a moment of affection.

Then we pull back and disengage. Emma is gone, running into the living room to re-enter the game she was playing. Gemma and I look at each other. I try looking farther and deeper into a place we have gone before. But I can't. At least, not now. All I can do now is get to a place of faith. It is with faith that I watch Gemma go back into the living room to be with Emma.

I wander the house, not knowing what I should be doing. Writing? Cleaning? Phoning? Packing? Planning? Biking?

It is with faith that I get dressed, carry my bicycle up from the basement, and head to Tater Lane. This is a hill that makes my legs understand, beyond a shadow of a doubt, that they are legs.

I pedal down to the first rise as fast as I can. It takes me ten minutes to reach the bottom of Guilford Street Extension: this has been the first warm-up. A sharp, right turn onto the flat approach to Tater Lane and I am beginning to tremble with anticipation. I sit up straight on the seat and begin a deeper breathing, an expansion into the lower haunts of my lungs, bones, and muscles. I've got fifteen minutes to get the oxygen-filled blood pumping out into every cell in my body. I tighten my spine and my abdominal muscles, centering my power in the core of my body, using the instructions I received from that really bad *Pilates for Dummies* video. OK. I am ready to start up Tater Lane.

The first hill is the second warm-up. By the time I reach the crest, which softly turns to the west, my muscles are primed. From this place in the road, a rider could be fooled into think-

ing that the rest of Tater Lane is now going to be like this: a
gently rising road of sweet curves bordered by fragrant woods.
Not so. One more curve a quarter mile up and the real Tater
Lane introduces itself to who you thought you were as a rider.
It is during the introduction, as you look up and up and up,
that you seriously question your ability to make it.

I am on the Gentle Slope of Deception, already imagining
the face of Father Tater Lane, when I see a deer. It is a small
one, charging out of a swampy low land onto the dirt road in
front of me. It appears as if it has been dropped from the sky.
It stands without flinching for a few seconds, looking forward
into the far woods, and then turns to see what might be
around. It spots me and stops moving, to really take a look at
me. I jump off of my bike; we are both stopped now. I don't
know which one of us will move first. We have stopped and
our eyes have met. I hold onto this connection for as long as I
am able—then we move. I think the deer moves first. I'm not
sure. The deer runs full on into the trees, not hesitating and
not stopping to look back.

I can't move then. I don't want to. I will never move from
this place and the light now left on the dirt where the deer
was. I stare at the light left there, a round shape. I think I can
still hear the deer—bounding off into the woods that it must
know so well by now. I could probably see it if I moved, but I
can't. I cannot get my legs to do anything.

Then a car comes from behind and forces my next motion;
I am back up on my bike, moving out of the car's way and
heading up Tater Lane, my body lagging behind my mind's

capacity to envision the hill already conquered. I charge up the hill on pure inspiration, fueled by the energy of seeing the light, the deer in sunlight, and the look in its eyes. I reach the impossible forty-five degree crest—the last gasp of hill. I'm not sure I can make it, the hill looming more like ninety degrees in front of me. It's a veritable wall. I swear to myself that whether I make it by bike or foot, my life will continue. We will close on our new house in Westminster West. We will finish packing in time. We will have enough money for the renovations. I will find my way back to Gemma like hummingbirds who always find their way back to each other in the spring, and I will come to love Emma.

It is with some kind of surrender to the hill, partnered with determination that compels me to reach the top of Tater Lane, my lungs pounding with the final blast of oxygen. I take in as much air as my lungs are capable of absorbing, gasping over the handlebars, sweat forming a soft layer of moisture on my skin. I will not get off this bicycle now that I have reached the peak, no matter what. I will stay pushing against the peddles— all of me on this bicycle with not a speck of me left back there on the sharp spine of Tater Lane. There is only flat road stretched out in front of me now. Looking behind me, the hill no longer looks like a forty-five degree angle but more like thirty degrees, slanting down, dark and away.

Through heaving breaths, I smile, saliva spilling over my lips. I can't swallow or lick. The flat road stretches on and out as my legs come back to me. I am suddenly full of wind and the desire to reach South Street as fast as I can. I would not go back for anything. I would not fly down Tater Lane in a free-fall. I will always come up Tater Lane, through the hard breaths, into the screaming heart that knows nothing else, into the joyful heart that knows what life is.

When I get home, Emma and Gemma are where I left them, together in the living room, working on an art project. I smile at them. They smile back. Emma's smile is still an unknown to me, full of lights and shadows, expressions that tease and hide whatever she might be feeling. Gemma's smiles are familiar. This smile looks like she has been caught by surprise, like she didn't know my entrance could still surprise her. I stand and watch the two of them a few seconds before I go upstairs to shower and change.

The first time I had encountered one of Gemma's surprised smiles was on a trip we took to southwestern Arizona a year after Danielle died. Each of us was in need of some parched earth and dry winds—there had been too much wetness; we were both grieved out from crying and surviving a particularly rabid winter in Vermont.

We covered a lot of ground, beginning in Albuquerque, New Mexico, making our way up to the Ring of Fire near Taos, then to Flagstaff, Arizona, and ending in Sedona, Arizona. Home of supposed energy vortices, red sand formations, and high-priced restaurants, we stayed a few days, watching the sun rise and become the protagonist each morning; the sun was definitely the main character out here in the desert.

One of those mornings, we got up earlier than the sun and

headed for a canyon hiking spot, famous for its views and wildlife. Supplied with a backpack filled with water, grapes, and trail mix, and fashioned with shorts, bandanas, t-shirts, boots, and lots of sunscreen, we set out on the well-marked trail. Back over the crusty heights, behind Gemma's head as she receded in front of me, the air was running in cross currents—in waves it blurred the features of the landscape so it all looked like it was inside an oven, even at this early hour of the day. It was hard to keep my eyes moist enough to withstand the blasts from the sand. I thought I saw, what appeared to be, starlings flying up and out of Gemma's hair but I didn't think starlings lived around here and the forms that looked like starlings soon dispersed into shifting waves of black and gray, becoming nothing more than vapor images, tricks played between eye and brain.

Gemma was wearing new, tanned, cowhide hiking boots, extremely fashionable but not practical. She knew better than to break them in out here on a desert hike but fashion and the lack of anything else to wear won out over comfort. She looked like a model from The Territory Ahead. On our second encounter, just a little over two years previous to this hike, Gemma had worn a mid-calf-length pink raincoat, collar swept up around her neck. She was uninhibited and confident in her clothes and body that night. The black and white, gold, royal pink elegance of her was breathtaking as she walked across the street, away from me, vanishing into a hotel lobby after a late afternoon lunch. In that vanishing, all that grace set against the white tiled walls of the hotel lobby, Gemma stirred a frenzied desire in me that turned into an adolescent-like obsession. For perhaps a month, my eager pursuit made Gemma question my mental condition; she asked mutual friends if I was a stalker. It took lots of reassurance from friends and lots of backing off from me to assuage Gemma's fears. She was calmed; we continued our courtship, finding an eventual, if not tenuous, balance between passion and reality.

We reached what seemed to be the end of the trail after an hour of hiking. We were above the desert floor on red cliffs rising up hundreds of feet with amazing views toward the north. Rock slabs had been laid down for people to sit on beneath the partial, ineffectual shade of some small pine trees. We sat drinking water and eating trail mix and grapes. An arid, hot wind was sweeping up at us from the desert sands and cool air was blowing from behind us from the hills. My skin didn't know what to do: rise up into gooseflesh or sweat.

Suddenly, from the depths of the desert, blown up on the currents of heated wind, there appeared a hummingbird. It rose until it was face to face with Gemma. It ignored me, hovering in front of Gemma for at least two minutes. Neither Gemma nor I moved. I watched the hummingbird and Gemma do their communing—faces vivid in their contrasting silhouettes, the air throbbing all around them.

While I watched, I wondered about Gemma and hummingbirds. Hummingbirds always found her and they always came really close to her as if trying to remember something about her or perhaps trying to figure out who she was. Gemma always remained so still, looking directly into the eyes of the

hummingbirds in a state of total recognition and acknowl-
edgment.

This particular hummingbird became sated; it gave a
small squeak and flew off, back down into the vaulting winds
from below. Gemma closed her eyes, turned to me, and
smiled. It was a smile that I was seeing for the first time during this trip. At least I thought I had never seen this smile before. Maybe it was the back lighting of the burnt sienna hills
and azure skies that simply made this smile seem brand new
to me. It appeared to be a smile beyond all judgment and
doubt, a free smile, one that took her away from her analyti-
cal mind.

It was through the appearance and disappearance of this
smile that I learned to gage the state of our relationship. When
Gemma was smiling like this, we were good; we were solid.
These periods of connection came and went, just like our moments of passion. But ever since Emma arrived, we had been
experiencing these moments of smiles and passion less and
less. I knew this change in our relationship could come with
other kinds of circumstances, not just with the arrival of a
child, and that Emma was not to blame. I also knew that
Gemma and I had to get away alone together if we were to
keep the surprised smiles and the connecting passion.

A few weeks after our date at the Marina, Gemma and I are
able to get away to the Maine Coast for an overnight. Sitting
in the bathroom at the hotel in southern Maine, I'm ready to
split the day down the middle: walking the beach for the rest

of the morning and writing in the afternoon. Driving from Vermont, from our new home in the hills near the small town of Putney, Gemma and I slowly got used to the idea of spending a day and evening without Emma. It took me days of convincing Gemma that it would be all right to leave Emma with her parents for one night. They were visiting from Florida and in the middle of their week-long visit had offered to take care of Emma so we could get away. It seemed that everyone was ready for this to happen, except for Gemma, who didn't fully trust that her aging parents could handle Emma, especially if she missed us enough to have a breakdown. There was no way of knowing unless we tried, I argued, and if Emma became inconsolable, we would return home immediately.

By now, with nine months of living with us and with Tanya gone to yet another rehabilitation center, this one in Florida, Emma had pretty much settled into what had become her new and safe life. Her night terrors had subsided, she liked school in our small village, she loved our new house across from an orchard; she particularly loved her new bedroom. An October overnight at the ocean was a must for Gemma and me as far as I could see and so I had become insistent.

So here I am in the hotel room trying to reduce things, put things away, set things aside so I can see straight again, so I can walk the beach and then write. I stare at the beige walls that hold painting of sailboats—domestic sailboats, like cows—all wildness gone out of them. These grazing sailboats look glued to the surface of the water; they aren't going anywhere. The bedspreads beneath the eternally becalmed sail-boats are some kind of play on a seaweed theme, I'm reckoning. I mean, what else could they possible be? Strings of green, leaf-like vegetation heading up and over the pillows, down into the mattress.

The ocean just outside the door is real. It's alive. It's moving as if it has been an ocean for a long time now, maybe even forever. And really, that's the part that gets me. The doing-it-forever thing. Emma has become a doing-it-forever thing and I know it because I am missing her just four hours after saying goodbye. I can't stand it; I didn't want her to become a forever thing.

I hear the sound of the sea, up and back. There's another sound, too. I think it's a bird. Gemma thinks it's a catbird. But then we listen more closely; it's singing every song ever sung by a bird and it's mocking them all. It's probably been doing it forever. We stand on the balcony listening to the bird, trying to spot it among the branches of a maple tree. Its songs are accompanied by the song of the ocean's motion. As if using the rhythm the ocean has set, the bird's notes follow along, practically beat for beat.

"Better chee, better chee," it sings a melody I don't recognize—not that I know many birdcalls.

"I wish I could stop worrying about her," Gemma says.

"You will. This used to happen when we first left Basia overnight, remember?"

"But this is different. Emma is a child," Gemma says. "I'm gonna watch a little television to zone out. OK?" Gemma asks.

After a few more minutes of listening to the ocean and bird duet, I join Gemma for a mind-numbing hour (or was it three?) of television. We fall asleep in separate beds.

Sometime during the night, I wake and get into bed with Gemma. I can hear the ocean—it sounds close, like it is running right up against the hotel. There are only the sounds of the ocean now and Gemma's breathing, both close, entering my body with quiet, methodic insistence.

While we slept, our bodies softened, the bones beneath chest flesh cracking open, little hairline cracks appearing, surely not discernible by X-ray. Through the night we became reacquainted, legs and arms reaching out, not closing up in retreat or pushing away in rejection. As the ocean came toward us, we moved toward each other in a saltwater surge. As the sea was leaving its mark on the small gray-lit rocks, we were leaving lips, teeth, and fingers, labia, nipples, and sweat marks all over each other's body. We hadn't made love like this in months.

The forever of the sea. The forever of our desire for each other. These things heal and bring us back to our senses, which have been beaten into a passionless coma through too much attention spent on the details.

Give me the ocean.

Give me back my senses.

Give me back my heart.

It is not Emma who has taken these things from me, I know. It is up to me to see that they were never taken away from me in the first place.

On our way home, we stop to get some beach rocks to use in our garden and along the borders of our yard. The rocks are close enough for us to gather and carry to our car, parked alongside the beach. Bags of small, round gray pebbles and huge, twenty pounders. I hoist these large ones with a bit of trepidation, fearing someone will stop me and scream, "Rock thief!" What if everyone who came this way, snagged a rock or two for their attempt at landscape gardening creativity? There wouldn't be a rock left on the beach.

I point this out to Gemma who shrugs and says, "I don't think anyone minds."

I look at the rocks again, stretched out before my eyes in both directions, north and south. They go on and on. There are millions of them. Maybe billions. We are the only people shuffling off to our car with some. The beach will be fine without the few that we have taken.

As we begin the ride home, heavily laden with our stash of stones, I realize that I am completely relaxed. It's even all right with me to make pit stops, something I normally cannot bring myself to do once I've gotten in the car and started moving in the designated direction. Gemma has her hand on my thigh as I drive, the warmth of it reminding me of the closeness we shared last night and reassuring me that we will share it again. She turns to smile at me. It is a new smile, one that I am certain I will see again and again, and one that I will come to know well.

7
JANE WEST
TO THE RESCUE

While my sisters and I were mashing Ken's and Barbie's bodies together in our idea of feverish ardor in northern New Jersey, Gemma was saving the world with Jane West in northern Massachusetts. Her games could be aptly called: "Jane West Saves the Day, Again." Gemma invented disaster upon disaster to which Jane West would arrive, with competent zeal, ready for action. "Jane West is my name. Triage is my aim." Bus accidents. Plane crashes. Epidemics. You name it; Jane West was on the scene, knowing exactly what to do.

Each one of us follows a course set early and deep. It was clear from the days of Jane West Saves the Day, that Gemma would be called upon, time and again, to rescue those around her. The family member, who invariably needed the most saving, turned out to be Tanya. No surprises there.

8
THE CURVES
OF THE SPINE

We have primary and secondary curves that form as we swim within our mothers' bodies. Pushed in and folded upside down in fluid—warm, wet, and quiet—in silence the cells get started—the coding sending off each one to become a part of the whole: heart, lung, eye, toe, and spine. Comprehension of this process begs for the presence of a creator, but I do not believe in God. I believe in the fluid that holds the fiercely determined force of life as it takes shape over and over again, knowing exactly what to do and what to become.

In this fluid world, Emma once floated. She began to stretch out her fingers and toes, feeling them move and reach for existence. She danced and soared and trembled; she felt it all, sensing her mother's joy, fear, and anguish. There was only liquid between the void and existence. Her senses developed: touch, taste, sight, sound, and smell with liquid as conductor, bringing the messages from beyond the boundaries of flesh. Through liquid she heard the owls that cried from the tops of the palm trees across the street. Through liquid she felt the heat and choking humidity of tropical sun and rain. She began to wait for the shadows her mother and father created as they passed over, not yet understanding whom those shadows belonged to or what kinds of harm shadows can bring. There were the raised voices and the shifts in volume and pace of her mother's heartbeat. Emma reached for that heart, as close as the next room, as far away as a dream that was fading as the morning swooped in, full of daylight.

When she was held tight to her own mother's chest as an infant, she did not find that original rhythm; something had changed. All throughout her childhood, she would throw off blankets and sheets, always moving, always restless. This jangling tension that forces her course through every moment will never cease. She will always be checking over her shoulder, looking for the shadows which used to inhabit her world of liquid. She will always be using her hands to create things, now it is fairy houses and forts in the woods. Emma will fidget. She will run and dance. She will talk and talk and talk, smashing silence into pieces that can be danced through.

We slow our pace down long enough to experience the curves of our spines fitting with the curves of another. Our bodies stretch out, long and limitless and our bones stop aching. The curves of our spines find their perfect roundness.

Back to back, with someone we have allowed in, we find a fit, our flesh moving in first, toward and into the flesh of another. Our spines: each vertebrae, transverse process, disc, and column sinks and let's go. The curves draw back and around while we sleep, shifting until they are almost exactly aligned with our lovers.

This happens if we are lucky and able to recognize, without thinking, that it is finally here: the rhythm of existence. Our hands seek out thighs, lips, hair, chest, arms, hands, and breath and all the liquids. We are ferocious in our desire to get in and close to the heart. If we can stop ourselves from thinking too long and hard, we allow our lovers to seek everything in us without running away or becoming afraid of what might be taken away. We find what we started reaching for when we were floating in uteri, and when we find it, up from the base of our spinal columns arises a cry. We can be taken for mad then, but our lovers will understand and cry, too. If we are lucky, neither one will devour the other and we will find what we have both been looking for—the curves of the spine and the rhythms those curves can create.

The rains have finally stopped. I am alone with Basia. Gemma took Emma to visit Tanya at the prison where she is doing time for attempting to rob the convenience store with Zucchini. Nabbed at an airport in Florida, Tanya must now pay the proverbial piper. I didn't want Emma to go and see Tanya. I don't want Emma to love Tanya or have the desire to see her. I want Emma to reject her mother so that Tanya will be punished for what she has done. But, of course, it is not up to Emma to punish her mother because I want her to. Tanya will always be Emma's mother, their love a primal and primordial force. All I can do is keep breathing, in and out, hoping to allow Emma passage on toward the rhythms she seeks—the rhythms that have nothing to do with the rhythms I can provide: the rhythms of her mother's love and of future lovers, friends, and close companions.

In the majority of moments when I am holding her, I stay trapped in my head where resistance and self-protection sing their battle chants. In these moments I am mostly incapable of hearing anything else, but sometimes the sound of Emma's heartbeat rises faintly, moving up close to my heart—she curls up and I can fit all of her within my arms. For the briefest time, she is all I hear, all I know.

Emma did not come from within my body but nestled in close to my body now, she is becoming a part of me. In these moments, I surrender to my growing love for her. Curve to curve, heartbeat to heartbeat, we are creating a rhythm together, a rhythm all our own.

9
THE "A" WORD

*M*y eyes open slowly. This early morning light is subdued and gray. I smell rain; it must have started during the night, probably a soft rain, without fanfare, without lightning or thunder or heavy driving walls of water. A spring rain. New rain.

Gemma is asleep next to me. In our new home for six months; we've survived our first winter, perched now on the edge of a spring that promises discoveries, like the stream down the southern slope of our four acres, the orchard across the dirt road, the three perennial gardens, the woods behind the house, the new neighbors.

I watch Gemma as she sleeps, her face goes from placid, a death-like mask, to twitching lips and brow. She looks troubled—waves of worry overtaking her features, as she encounters adversaries from the deep. I know that one of those adversaries is me. We are heading toward a risky place—the exploration of the word: "adoption"; Gemma and I have been swinging around it these last few months. Like monkeys, she and I have been clinging to our own personal vine. We get closer and closer to each other and the tree, which is supporting us. It feels like a crash is imminent.

I'm sure that Gemma has been thinking about adopting Emma ever since she landed with us, over a year ago now. I'll bet she's even inquired about the process and talked about it with a well chosen few. I am certain she has been formulating her strategy—similar to one a lawyer must create in order to convince a jury to convict or acquit a suspected criminal. She knows that I will block her initial attempt to make a case for adoption. I have demonstrated through actions, and sometimes words, that I do not want the responsibility of parenthood. Gemma knows my family history and how it continues to shape my decisions: as the oldest of five sisters with a mentally debilitated mother who finally left when I was eight and a half, I had to step into a care-giving role, one I did not necessarily want. Although our father was exemplary in making sure we had what we needed (he was especially good at providing us with unconditional love in great measure), being the older sister in charge was, at times, a confusing burden. I knew what I had to do, saw it in front of me at all times but I also wanted to turn and run from what was being asked of me. But I did not balk or shirk from my responsibilities until much later. My rebellion started when I was in my early twenties. By then I believed I was through with having to be in a pivotal and primary care-giving role. I did not think that I would ever have to fight with myself, or anyone else, about taking on the responsibilities of raising a child or children. Becoming a teacher and an aunt allowed there to be a comfortable and guaranteed distance between me and a direct hook-up to main parental squeeze. It was perfection. Still connected to the oldest sibling-in-charge skills I had organically acquired, the roles of teacher and aunt fit me the way sweatpants and a T-shirt did.

Being with kids in a teaching capacity is a reflex—like an involuntary muscle contraction or heartbeat. Whether it's one-on-one or in large groups, I am comfortable. It usually takes me a few seconds to size up a kid or group of kids for the best way to make an approach, what their overriding needs are, and what disciplinary tactics will work most effectively. Most often, my opening involves self-effacing humor or a benevolent bantering routine, similar to, or how I would like to believe, the approach a stand-up comedienne might make in a similar situation. Exaggerated facial contortions and over-the-top guttural utterances are a sure-fire technique. Jim Carrey's and Whoopi Goldberg's big teeth spring to mind. Jon Stewart's tie-straightening routine rides the back of my mind as I stretch my face into expressions absolutely certain to melt the most suspicious and cynical children. It's size 'em up and make them laugh, disarming them, maybe even dissolving a few of their defenses, so I can get on with the ultimate purpose of the interaction: trust, which will then lead to a shot at the absorption of some kind of knowledge or some kind of relationship connection. But no matter how close I get to a student or sib-ling's child, I can always send them back to their parents for the more messy and core, aspects of intimacy.

That is certainly what we did with Emma the first six years of her life, even when we sometimes knew sending her back to Tanya was not our preferred choice. And up until now, I believed we would be sending her back again, after Tanya's latest attempt at rehabilitation. The year and half of living with us, moving with us, and setting up a new home with us have stirred the whispering voices of the angels who guard the souls of children. It is becoming clearer and clearer as their voices grow louder, that the song they are singing has only one word in its chorus and that word begins with an "A."

As Tanya fades back into a manic retreat from full-time re-sponsibility for raising Emma, the din from the choir grows harder to ignore.

While a Law and Order Gang is dogging Tanya, the case for adoption is dogging me. If only adoption wasn't so danged per-manent. If only there could be some escape clause written into an adoption agreement. But I'm sure that is not how it works. And I am certain that it would be hard, if not impossible, to convince Gemma of the necessity for one. My struggle with ar-riving at acceptance is absurd, almost vile, and extremely un-attractive. Even though no one has come out and said it, I'm sure people (hordes of them) are thinking to themselves, "What's wrong with her? She's so great with kids, too. Such a shame. Such an awful, goldang, shame."

Of course, since Emma came to live with us, it seems that I am running into more and more people who have become responsible for raising their kinfolk's kids, whether they wanted to or not. This wouldn't be so bad, if not for the abhorrent fact that most of these people are glad, even grateful, for what most of them refer to as a "gift." These goody, goody, good Samaritans must be way better adjusted than I am or closer to some sort of beatific truth or they are just plain liars. Maybe my friend, Elaine, was right. Maybe it will take me at least three years to get used to the idea of raising Emma. But how long it will take to come to terms with adopting her, is anyone's guess.

When I listen to these high and mighty rescue workers, I have to remind myself to ask them if the kids they have taken in are blood relatives or not. My limited and, I suppose, biased, data reveal that people are way more inclined to accept a blood kin into their fold than take on a waif from outside the family, especially if that castoff arrived unexpectedly. Rationalization for my skewed and pitiful point of view. That always helps.

It is a blessed relief when I encounter or hear of someone in a similar predicament who is just as conflicted as I am.

"My sister is having to raise her brother's two kids because the brother went to prison for murdering the cable guy and driving over a manatee with a motorboat when he was trying to escape from a Law and Order Gang."

"Is she happy about it?" I ask with anticipation.

"Are you kidding? She's a wreck. She never wanted to have children. She was raised by some wacko mother, schizophrenic, I think, and some abusive father who died when she was nine and thought she would make a miserable parent. She's doing it because she is the only one capable of doing it."

"Is she getting any help? Support?"

"She's in some kind of support group for families who have given up their lives for relative's kids. She says it really helps. You might want to think about joining it."

Oh, for God's sake. A flippin support group? It's a little too soon for that. Maybe I'm wrong.

"You're wrong, Carol. It is not going to be that different from the way it is now. It's a legal issue. You know as well as I do that Tanya will probably never be capable of raising Emma. If she is ready someday, great. But for now, we've got to adopt her so we can make medical and legal decisions, get some financial support, and start creating a family for her. Really. It won't be any different than it is now."

"You're kidding, right? Not different? Gemma, adoption is way more different. It's serious. It's permanent. How is that not different? Permanent. It's permanent."

"Yeah? And your point?"

"It's permanent! How many more ways can it be said?"

Gemma looks at me, the Sicilian blood in her taking over every feature of her face. She's so beautiful when the blood rising into her face is hot, Mediterranean, and olive oil filled. Even when we are having this kind of head-to-head, heart-to-heart conflict, I am often arrested by her features, held breathless by the passionate movements of her lips and eyes. At moments, when transfixed this way by her, I become helpless, a limp and useless sparring partner.

"Darling, I'm sorry this is so hard for you but you know somewhere inside of you that this is what we have to do. Right?"

I know what my answer will be. The question that is riding right next to the words I am about to say is: "How long will it take me to sincerely believe it?"

"Yes, Gemma. I know."

From here, from this place of "we both know it's the right thing to do," comes all the decisions we must make about how to proceed with the adoption process. Gemma is already five steps into it with lists of potential lawyers, state officials we need to contact, and lists of the preliminary forms we must fill out to get this roller coaster moving. In the initial discussion that we have, Gemma volunteers to take on more of the tasks: phone calls, setting up appointments, completing the paperwork, and signing checks. I am a tag-along participant. Knowing that what we are doing is the right thing doesn't necessarily create an instant enthusiasm in me. And I'm sure it's got to be a drag on Gemma's momentum. She is so clear and so bull's-eye focused on the outcome that, for now, I give her free reign over every part of the process. There are times when she must secure, not only my OK, but my signature as well. Mostly, I find the dotted line and scrawl out my initials without protest. Big and swirling—almost defiant—my signature takes up a lot of room on the forms. Gemma's small, compact, and readable signature always seems to float either above or next to mine. These signatures of ours are graphic displays in contrasts, portraits of opposite energies. Even the way we go about writing our signatures is completely different.

Gemma holds the pen lightly—a gentle pressure of ink flowing out in neat little bursts filling the receiving line with precise loops and flaring strokes. It takes her maybe half a minute to sign her name because she writes out the whole thing. Every letter makes it in. When she is finished, Gemma looks it over to make sure it has all the dots, crosses, periods, and curls. Although I can render a fairly good facsimile of her signature, I can never come up with a perfect match. Gemma's signature is too fussy. I lose patience and usually wind up sending a letter tilting off too far to the right, the direction her letters lean toward. Signatures are all about angles and uniquely drawn lines of identity. There is a weight of personality that must strike the paper just so in order for it to successfully and perfectly represent the signer. Gemma is one hundred forty pounds of pure passion, coiled tightly inside, ready for task-oriented action. This force of hers is conveyed in her signature; at least I think it is, given my limited knowledge of signature analysis. You can intuit that she is finely creative, that she likes order, and that she wants you to know exactly who is doing the signing. There is a hint of mystery, but there is definitely no room for misinterpretation of purpose.

How to describe my own signature? As owner and executioner of the mess I make, it is obviously impossible to paint an objective picture of it. Simply put, it is a whirling smush of the three first letters of my three names. Take the "C," "A," and "O," and throw them together with impatience, one hundred fifty-five pounds of unleashed chaos, frustration over the lack of space provided for signatures (sometimes not even half an inch), topped off with the desire for whoever sees my signature to be impressed, and you have my signature. Unreadable. Large. Dramatic. As close to controlled as I can get it. Gemma's attempts at forging my scribbled CAO are actually quite impressive, but then, it's easier to mimic large and unreadable than it is to copy controlled and precise. You tell me.

So, we've narrowed the lawyer search down to two candidates: a lesbian and a non-lesbian. To be honest, we are basing our choice on credentials, relevant experience, and recommendation. Yes. Lesbian is probably a plus and I mean probably. Just because a lawyer is a lesbian doesn't mean she'll be dripping with understanding and compassion for our plight. Many a sweet-talking lesbian has turned up her nose at our situation, as if the whole thing is stinking and repugnant. This is no "Give us a lesbian lawyer or bail."

But as it turns out, we go with the lesbian lawyer. She's smart, experienced, and she's really tall, something that would intimidate even the most fiendish of criminals. (I'm thinking of Sam. We still don't know what he's capable of and need a big tall lesbian to scare him if he goes to the dark side.) She's organized (scored big points with Gemma). She wears fashionably droll blue or gray business suits. And she has a very dry, sarcastic sense of humor. She is rarely inclined to let her humor escape but when she does it is a wit worth waiting for. Gemma particularly appreciates dry and sarcastic. I'm a fan more of the adolescent male humor kind. *Monty Python and the Holy Grail* or Chris Rock's *Pootie Tang* are good examples of the fare I like. But, that doesn't mean I don't admire and approve of the drier, sarcastic side of humor.

At our first meeting with Pam (a lesbian name if I've ever heard one), it's all business, which, I guess, is a good thing. Every once in awhile, I try injecting a little levity, but neither Gemma nor Pam seem interested or particularly amused by these attempts. They must both feel this is not the time for stupid, inane humor. I can understand their desire to get on with the brutally serious task at hand but I also think it's good to laugh a little during the hard moments. OK. OK. I'll stop.

Pam asks every conceivable question about us — length of relationship, commitment intention, salaries, job security, home ownership, criminal records, driving records, number of parking tickets accrued over the years, assets, liabilities, trinkets, buried treasure, got a castle hidden away somewhere? Egads. We sure aren't squeaky clean but neither one of us knows where the bodies are buried either.

Our first meeting takes hours. As we end it, Gemma wisely asks Pam what her fee is going to be. "One hundred and fifty dollars an hour." This will be the last of the marathon meetings. Gemma gulps, not something she does often. "Are there any programs offering financial assistance for the lawyer fees?"

"Yes, there are, but with Carol's salary, I don't think you would qualify. I can check into it, though."

Forty-two thousand dollars a year puts me over the top? Who came up with the figures that make or break the lines of assistance? I'm positive it's not arbitrary, but when you're sitting in it, in the heap of trouble that you must wind up paying for, the heap you were not responsible for creating, it's hard to wrap your mind around the price that you must pay to come to the rescue. Gemma and I are coming to the rescue and we must pay, too? Something about this equation does not make sense. Gemma plus Carol plus Emma equals PAY UP? We cannot ask Tanya for financial assistance—she never has money, always borrowing from her parents. We cannot ask Gemma's brothers; they have families and troubles of their own. My family? Sure. There might be a buck or two but damn if I ask them for help with this. Looks like we are going to have to eat it.

"Is there some kind of payment plan?" Gemma inquires.

"Payment plan?" Pam looks at Gemma as if she's joking, as if she's never heard of such a thing. What? Pam has never experienced lean times? Hate to think it about a fellow lesbian, but I'm beginning to think Pam is from the privileged side of the tracks. Trust fund baby? Endowment? Inheritance? Whatever it is, she seems unable to comprehend our predicament.

"You know, where we pay a bit at a time?" Gemma continues.

"You mean an 'installment plan'?"

"Yeah, installments." Duh. Call it whatever you like, lesbian lawyer Pam. We cannot pay the fees all at once. Got it? A light begins to rise up in her eyes—an awakening of long lost concepts or images recalled from the nightly news broadcast about bums living on skid row.

"Yes. Yes. Of course. We can make arrangements for payments that you can afford."

Oh, really. Thanks, Pam. I honestly can't believe she is beyond all this. Maybe all the years spent lawyering have turned her into the legalese lawyer she has become. Or maybe she is so super-focused on the details of our case, she just didn't see financial burden coming. OK. I'll give her that. Dear Pam, forgive me.

Pam goes over the figures, trying to come up with a number that Gemma and I can head toward. Ten thousand dollars, minimum. This covers fees, paperwork, court hearings, transportation (of whom?), judge fees, research fees, and closing costs. (We are not buying a house.) I look at Gemma. She is nodding her head, very slowly, like in a very bad movie, where slow-mo is used as a last ditch effort to make the movie more interesting and new-age indie-like. Now what? We could each sell our bodies. Street price in rural Vermont? Gemma shakes her head—wake up! We have nowhere else to go but forward, financial burden or no financial burden. We'll have to make this work. Gemma finally turns toward me, her face a straight-on, direct hit of purpose. I catch it and nod. No misinterpretation here. We'll do it, no matter what the cost. I can only hope that as I nod my head, I know what the heck it is I'm agreeing to.

"Did you know it was going to cost this much?" I ask Gemma once we are in the car, away from the cold cucumber countenance of Pam.

"Yeah. I knew. No. I had no idea, OK.? What would you like me to say?"

"Just what you said. It's fine. We'll deal with it."

"That's what you always say, Carol. How will we deal with it?"

"The installment plan, of course?"

"Is she for real? It's like she never heard of such a thing. Are we crazy or stupid?"

"Naïve, I guess."

"Honey. Really. How are we going to pay for all of this?"

"A buck at a time." It's the best I can come up with.

Pam is efficient. She's cool. Suave. Dependable. Everything a lawyer should be. She gathers the information—probes, sniffs it out, and finds the holes and weaknesses in our case. There aren't many according to her. We are upstanding citizens, proven pillars of our community. The fact that Tanya is so willing (even enthusiastically inclined) to give us legal custody of Emma, establishes a very strong argument in our favor. Pam sees clear sailing, maybe even a slam-dunk. The ten thousand dollars estimate for costs is instantly cut in half. This could be a no-brainer. Prove that we are competent. Get the signatures from the parents relinquishing their rights, pay the costs (installment plan, of course), and away we go to the judge for final approval.

Ready. Set. STOP.

We didn't count on the wrath and refusal of Sam. In the time it takes for him to say, "No," the process of adoption comes to a halt. It will probably take at least a month to get the state of Florida to send us Sam's criminal records. And then it will take another month for Pam to go through them and come up with a case against him. Then it will take another month to get permission to transport him from Florida to Vermont. Maybe another month to set up the court hearing dates. So, in about four months, we should be able to face Sam, argue our case in front of a judge, receive the decision, and continue on with the adoption proceedings. What are we supposed to do in the meantime? "Don't get a parking ticket, whatever you do," counsels Pam, our lawyer supreme.

10
DO THE RIGHT THING

*L*ook at him. Just look at him. In all his sinister glory, Sam looks up at Gemma and me from the black-and white photograph that the state of Florida sent to our lawyer when she requested his criminal records. Head shorn and face expressionless, except for the eyes, which are filled with the long shadows of demons that certainly must haunt his dreams, these two photos instantly flood me with sad terror. Incredible. This can't be Emma's father.

Criminal records had to be obtained because Sam will not give up his parental rights to Emma. Just shy of two years since Emma and Tanya lived with Sam in Florida, he still holds onto the dream of a future with them. This dream must surely mark the time he has left in prison. He probably draws an "x" through each completed day on a wall calendar, which hangs

next to photographs of Tanya and Emma. He boasts of Emma
to his cellmate — "She's beautiful and smart. Blue eyes, just
like her old man. Ain't that right, Wayne?" They laugh and
light cigarettes. Then Sam sits down to write another letter to
Emma and while he's at it, he will write one to Gemma and
me, telling us where to get off, thinking we could take his precious, baby girl from him. We've got another thing coming.
God wants Emma to have a mommy and a daddy, not a
mommy and a mommy. Perverts. He's gonna do his time, get
his act together, and then come and get Emma.

That may be his idea of the right thing to do, but it is not
anyone else's, not even Tanya's, who, by now, has signed away
her legal rights to Emma. I have to think that must have been
almost as difficult an act of surrender for Tanya as handing
Emma over to us that January afternoon, only now she has
had more time to think about it and the implications this decision promises. Then again, maybe it was a relief; the responsibilities inherent with being a parent have been lifted
from her. Tanya can settle back and really grieve now. She
can thrash and gnaw at the insides of her cheeks in tortured
anguish. It's the kind of relief that drug addicts and alcoholics
love to wallow in. If this doesn't send her back to cocaine, then
perhaps she's got a chance of having some kind of relationship with Emma. Tanya has seen the light — now, she must
make Sam see it, too.

She writes him a letter, asking him to change his mind
about giving up his right. At least, that's what we think she

does. We don't actually see the letter she has written. Does she really understand this game of high stakes? Do any of us?

I watch from my partner vantage point as Gemma rises up into fierce bear form as the fight with Sam grows in intensity. The harder the fight, the more focused she becomes. For the most part, I feel as if I am being directed by her storm of energy; I am doing as I am told, accompanying her as she suits up for the next round in the ring. This would be a perfect time to ditch. But I know in my bones that if I backed out now, it would certainly be the end of my relationship with Gemma and, subsequently, Emma. There have been decisive moments all along the way, when bailing could have happened without a whole lot of fanfare. And Gemma would have fought on, sword blazing, without looking back. I know that I am not insignificant in all of this. As Gemma wields her flashing blade, I stand beside her so she is not alone, I help her to sleep each night, my hot body furnishing the heat her cold one needs. I am her comic relief and venting rag. I know that I am Emma's "Kiki" and Gemma's big love, but I also know that they could do this without me.

Right now, we must prepare to do battle with Sam. Here is another deciding moment—a place for me to take stock and either hang in there with Gemma and Emma or turn tail and run. The lines are drawn. Sam replies to Tanya that no way will he give away his rights. So now, court hearings must be scheduled and transportation for Sam must be arranged. Evidence must be gathered which will be used to make the case against Sam. Although is seems obvious that Sam is not a re-liable—much less safe—person for Emma to be raised by, a case must be made proving this. It will take commitment, focus, and lots of money.

It's right around this time of digging into pockets and see-through bank accounts that another layer of resentment set-tles like colored sand in my glass jar of a heart. Why must we pay for everything? Why isn't Tanya being asked to fund some of the adoption costs? Gemma seems determined not to ask Tanya for anything, claiming she does not want to owe her or feel obliged to her in any way. So, it must be buck up, suit up, and step up.

I am looking for a warrior. If she exists, I am not aware of her presence within me. All I can find is a capitulating wimp who lets her Sicilian partner take the heat and accusations. I can stand by Gemma's side all right. Sometimes I am even capa-ble of flashing a monster glare or two, but lead the troops? I've tried. As my father would say, "It doesn't come off."

I have always hoped that just the mere appearance of my five-feet-nine-inch frame, blue eyes set boldly forward in a deadly stare would be enough to thwart an enemy. I look at the photograph of Sam and have to acknowledge that any attempt at combating him needs to be undertaken by an expert— someone who knows her stuff through and through, prefer-ably someone with Latin blood running in her veins. That ain't me, babe. Gemma, with her hot Italian lineage and I, with my Germanic ice chip heritage, fall into our battle roles without thinking. Although we would like it to be different at times, we intuitively know this is the only course of action. Perhaps some day we will not struggle with each other over it—we will spend our energy simply doing what we do well. Fighting with each other only saps what little reserve we have to combat the real adversaries. We need what we have to attack those who would cause us real harm, in this case: Sam. We must gather up what strength we have and step to the front together. I wish it weren't so hard.

We meet with our lawyer to plan the strategy. With Sam's photograph and letters of defiant response placed in the center of the table, she lays out the possible courses of attack. Each one seems full of risks. We find out more about Sam's criminal history. This guy has spent more time in the slammer than out. No surprise here. But this certainly ups the stakes. Sam is clearly incapable of making a decision based on sound and realistic thinking. Who is he turning to for counsel? His cellmate? A state-appointed lawyer? In Sam's next letter, we find out it's someone a lot of people consider to be "above the law."

I have nothing against God. If I could, I would believe there was some sweet old geezer in a place called "Heaven" watching out for me and those I care about. The comfort and peace of mind inherent in such a belief would be welcomed. But over the years, of deep living, replete with great grief, suffering, and joy, I have lost what I consider to be a fearfully desperate need to believe in a being that created and continues to monitor our world. I am open to the existence of what I call a "life force," which is a kind of supernatural substance bonding us all together and moves beyond our ability to perceive it. This life energy runs through everything and perhaps when our physical bodies give out, the life energy, which has fueled our existence, simply moves back out into the greater expanse. But consciousness beyond death? Heaven? Hell? Baby Jesus? Immaculate Conception? Father God? I don't buy it.

But apparently, in one of Sam's more introspective and remorseful moments, he does buy it and becomes "Born Again." So now he's got GOD on his sorry-ass side. Two "lesbian whores" are no match for a convicted criminal who has accepted Baby Jesus as his personal savior. His god obviously thinks Gemma and I are not worthy of raising Emma, little gift from HIM that she is. The letters that Sam now sends are filled with endless claptrap about God's plan for Sam, Tanya, and Emma. It's God's will that they be together again, in His name, amen. Case closed.

Now we are really screwed. How do we knock sense into a pigheaded blowhard who believes God is watching his back? Our lawyer sits at the conference table shaking her head from side to side. Yup, we're screwed.

We can go no further toward adoption. We are in the land of halfway there. Although we have guardianship of Emma, there are restrictions; she is still Tanya and Sam's child. Certain medical and legal decisions can only be made by them. Tanya is about to go back to Arizona with a man she met at a rehabilitation center there. We cannot be left here in mid-fight. Tanya will be asked to testify against Sam at the court hearing and that is something we are sure she doesn't want to do. Tanya, more than anyone else, knows what Sam might be capable of when pushed against a wall. We get her to stay long enough to write one more pleading letter to Sam, a down-on-her-knees letter. When the emphatic "NO!" comes back from Sam, our lawyer moves into high gear, scheduling mode, putting the pieces in place for the hearing. She also advises us to contact the police and set up a restraining order against Sam, just in case he makes good on his threats to come and take Emma in the night.

Maybe Sam was cute once. Maybe sweet in disposition. Maybe his momma actually showered him with loving kindness and read him *Goodnight Moon* each night. At what point did he go so far off the beam that he could begin to consider and then act out such sinister plots as armed robbery or kidnapping? How can he justify these actions to the God he professes to love and receive guidance from? I spend some time contemplating Sam's fall from grace, trying to find some compassion and understanding for the guy. But then I imagine him paying someone to come to Vermont, finding us, kidnapping Emma, and murdering Gemma, me, and Basia as we lay sleeping in our beds. Empathy and compassion fly right out the window facing southwest and into the woods beyond. I want this guy dead. Maybe we can get someone to kill him — with all the Northern Jersey Italians that I know from my childhood spent growing up in Fort Lee, New Jersey; surely one of them must be an assassin or have family ties to one. I wonder how much it would cost. Desperation and fear certainly drive us to imagine despicable yet understandable things.

"This has gone way too far," Gemma proclaims after she hears my latest plans to have Sam bumped off. "He must have some sense of decency." I look at her with raised eyebrows and contorted smirk. "No, really. I'm going to write him a letter. Just lay it out for him. At this point, it certainly can't do any harm."

Gemma jumps to the front lines again. By now, I know that her Greatest Strength (at least the one I am the most in awe of) is her ability to communicate straight on through to the core of any matter. Her letter is a shining testament to that ability. She sends it and we wait.

Three weeks later, we receive the long-anticipated phone call from our lawyer.

"I don't know how you did it, Gemma. The papers came back, signed. Are you ready for Phase 2?" Our lawyer's voice had never sounded so light and frothy.

Sam's release date from prison has come and gone. We found out that he received a hefty financial settlement from the state of Florida for asbestos poisoning. While working on a construction project within the prison, he was exposed to enough of the tiny glass slivers to seriously damage his lungs. For a few months before his release, Sam promised to send a hunk of the money for us to open a bank account for Emma. I guess being released from prison makes you forget all kinds of promises. The newly acquired freedom must have gone directly to his twitching trigger fingers. We have never received a cent from Sam nor have we heard a word.

Emma talks about wanting to see him again someday. I look at the few photographs she has of him. Young, compact, wearing bad-boy jeans, leather jacket, and sporting long hair tied back into a ponytail, he looks hopeful, ready for anything.

I no longer wish Sam harm. I don't really think about him enough to wish much of anything for him. I do wish that whatever life he has chosen to live these past five years, he is content enough to stay far away from us. Until Emma is older and is capable of deciding that seeing him again would be safe and worth the risks, I hope he continues to do the right thing.

11
EMMA HAS TWO AUNTIES

*G*emma and I are behaving ourselves admirably as we sit in the two soft armchairs facing the social worker assigned to interview us. This is the first of possibly four meetings; two will be held at our home so she can see, up close and way personal, if our home environment is a suitable one for raising Emma. She wants to know everything about us, including the sordid tales of our childhoods. Why? I suppose in case there are any glaring red-flag traumas or behaviors that might indicate a pathology that could rear up and put Emma at risk. How safe are we two? Cindy is going to find out. She's on the hunt and she is very clever at it.

Cindy is unmasking us, bit by bit, with a smile that seems to be made of gossamer thread. Each time she smiles, I let loose with another story from my past. Why she started with me, we will never know. About twenty minutes into my story, which is replete with the tragedies that have befallen my family, Gemma clears her throat loudly. The sound startles me and snaps me out of my self-involved monologue. Suddenly embarrassed, I sputter out, "God! I've gone on and on about myself. I'm sorry. I didn't mean to say so much about my life."

Cindy waves me off with a gentle flutter of her hand. "This has been great. You have had a very interesting life."

"She loves talking about it. She even wrote a book about it," Gemma volunteers. I am not sure if Gemma is being gracious and proud of this fact or facetious and mortified. I study her face for clues. We stop so Cindy can write down the name of my book. Then she turns to Gemma and says, "We'll get to your story next time. Is that all right with you?"

"Sure," Gemma says with some relief.

At the next meeting, Gemma spills her family beans all over Cindy's office. She actually talks way longer than I did. It is obvious that Gemma needs this wringing out of the family dirty washcloth. I have never heard her explain the family dynamics and dysfunction with such accuracy and sentiment. It is so poignant that I start getting choked up, tears beginning to run down my face. Good Lord, Gemma has had it rough. That ridiculous family of hers, always expecting her to save them, fix everything, and be the goddamn adult.

Cindy keeps nodding, with an entirely convincing look of rapt attention. Being someone who has to muster great will to stay focused on what other people are saying (mostly), I am amazed by Cindy's display. Obviously she has learned her social work skills well and honed them to a fine art. I wonder if she has to consciously remind herself to stay present or whether the years of "active listening" have become assimilated into her being so completely that, by now, it comes naturally. I'm guessing that she is about sixty years old. Chances are she has been doing this kind of work for many years; her demeanor of quiet concern seems extremely genuine. This act is no ruse.

I turn to watch Gemma as she digs down deeper into the lower layers where there are no explanations, just the unfiltered truth. Maybe if I really listen, I can hear Gemma without connecting the dots so that what she is saying leads directly to me. Maybe then I will learn something new, an insight that would deactivate the automatic reaction buzzer that Gemma's words often push, which either makes me feel badly because I can't help her or badly because whatever she is saying is really a condemnation of my actions. But getting out of my own way is easier talked about than actually achieved. Today's revelations are no different. I sit squirming in the armchair.

Gemma speaks about that day on the beach in Nova Scotia—a pre-Emma moment. We knew Tanya was pregnant then. We were filled with a living dread of the birth and not because we loathed children, obviously. Gemma found a tiny stone on the beach. The seas had done some etching—it had what Gemma interpreted to be a miniature smiley face carved into it. Holding the stone up to the skies, Gemma prayed to the little face, begging it not to come through. She explained how hard it would be to emerge into this family and that she would be better off staying put in the stratosphere. Then she added, "But if you have to come, I promise to help you."

If there are messages that make it through the walls that separate us from the void, then I'm betting one was conveyed to the baby forming within Tanya's womb. Whether she received both parts of Gemma's entreaty and promise remains moot. It doesn't really matter now: Emma was born.

Sometimes I believe Emma is the only one capable of taking on this clan of Sicilians, showing them how to reach across judgment, fear, and resistance long enough to see that whoever is on the other side, they are not the enemy. I do not believe that she was sent here by some supreme being. But perhaps there are lines of communication that we cannot perceive, streams of collective consciousness that pick up and deliver, what we call "prayers." If light waves and sound waves exist, beams that we cannot see or hear with our physical senses until they reach our sphere of reality, then why not communication beams? Maybe Emma received a communication beam from Gemma on that cool morning in May, five months before her arrival.

When Gemma wants to get through to someone, she gets through; there is no escaping the focus and power of her will to communicate. I have seen Gemma go up against the crustiest of old codgers, completely disarming them. Neighbors who lived on the other side of a duplex wall swore they could feel Gemma's energy (wrath) right through the plaster. If she has enough volts to propel messages through wood, plaster, and metal, I believe the likelihood that she can break through dimensions is pretty high.

I am thinking about Gemma's extraordinary powers as she speaks to Cindy. The new insight comes, but it is not what I had expected. I can see that Gemma needs someone to listen to her, really listen to her. I can do this. I've been listening to her for twelve years now. I just need to listen better.

"Are you listening to me?" Gemma asks later that day as we process the meeting with Cindy.

"I thought I was," I reply, puzzled.

"You don't look like you are really listening," she jabs back.

Oh great! Now I suppose there are degrees of listening, subtle dead giveaways that indicate whether I am actually fully engaged or not. How did Gemma know I was thinking about the bike ride I wanted to take before it gets too dark? Somehow, she's onto me. When did Cindy have the chance to pull Gemma aside and give her a lesson in the art of Partner Listening Skills Detection? It must've been when I went to the bathroom.

"I was listening. You were saying how important it is for you to be acknowledged, especially when you are talking about feelings having to do with your family." I smile after my declaration of proof positive. It's a smile that my sisters and I perfected when we were children and had to convince all the adults around us that we were OK, even when we actually were not OK. Unless someone is particularly astute at seeing

past the smile/grimace, they are duped, and therefore, satisfied that all is well. I have forgotten how many times I have
used this tactic on Gemma, with only moderate success.

"I hate that smile. It makes me feel like this is all a big joke
to you. Can you just listen without making a big deal out of it?
That's all I'm asking."

Didn't she hear me? I was listening, even if it didn't meet
her High Standards of Listening Protocol.

I want to say, "STOP! Can't we be done for the day? Hasn't
there been a suitable amount of processing?" But I don't say it.
The fact remains that Gemma and I will always have very different ways of coming to terms with anything difficult and
challenging. Gemma will process through words, through that
critical, analytically leaning mind. I will bike, walk, or even
crash through it, with my impulsive, impatient dash to the next
thing, quick. Ne'er the twain shall meet. What in the world
were we thinking when we took this adoption thing on?

We were thinking what a lot of other people were thinking:
that Gemma and I were a perfectly balanced couple, making
the perfect parents to raise Emma. Perhaps blinded by their
desire to have it work, these denizens of our peaceable hamlet state and restate encouraging words about how lucky
Emma is to have two such different aunties. We are the yin
and the yang. The organized and the chaotic. The salt and
pepper. The tomato and the tomahto.

It is the balancing act that Cindy sees the day she comes for
the first home visit. She sits at our dining room table, listening

her heart out. Emma moves between Gemma and me: back and forth, she plops on one lap, then the other. Basia circles; around and around the table, she helps to create a closed circuit. Cindy would have to be a block of ice not to feel the heat from our love. Even I am impressed with the family we're creating—here and now—this is what we truly are. I am seeing it clearly. We are a family. How and when did this happen?

"How do you like living with two Mommies?" Cindy asks Emma, who is sitting on Gemma's lap presently.

No one speaks. Gemma and I exchange the quickest of sideways glances. Who is going to tell her?

"Ah . . . Emma doesn't refer to us as her, 'Mommies.' She calls me, 'Kiki', and Gemma, 'Gigi.' She's been calling us by these names since she started to talk. Right, Emma?" I explain. I thought for sure we had told Cindy this already. "She still has a mommy."

"Oh yes. Forgive me. I have that written right here in my notes."

"That's OK. Lots of people do it," I offer.

"So, should I call Kiki and Gigi your aunties?" she asks Emma.

"Yep," Emma sinks deeper into Gemma's body.

"Are you feeling shy?" Gemma asks Emma very quietly.

Emma nods her head with her eyes riveted on Cindy's face. I'm hoping this home visit doesn't have to go on for too long. How many questions can Cindy possibly have to ask? Can't she see that the home we are providing is safe and warm and all cuddly and politically correct? Don't we look just like

the Cleavers? Well . . . except for the two aunties thing? I am
certain that Cindy's abuse radar is just as fine-tuned as her ability to listen actively. She can probably sense a battered kid the
second she walks into a house for a visit. There have to be
signs—furtive looks, jittery movements, skittish animals,
guarded words, tentative handshakes, and the smell of pain. I
look at the four of us sitting before our one-woman jury/judge.
The onus is on us to demonstrate that we are capable of raising Emma without bringing her harm. And it is up to Cindy
to see through to the truth of it. She will go back to her su-
pervisor and either fire the starting gate gun or send all play-
ers back to the locker room for a new game plan. So far, Cindy
comes across as someone who can see straight into the moti-
vations and intentions of perspective adoptive parents. Yes. We
are anxious, wary, and possibly a bit defensive, but as I'm betting Cindy can plainly see, we are dripping with sincerity.
Aren't we? Aren't I?

My eyes meet Cindy's. She smiles politely and impercep-
tibly raises her eyebrows. Uh-oh. My eyes meet Gemma's. She
doesn't smile, but she does raise her eyebrows. Wait a minute.
Has this visit been set up to decide whether I am committed
to the adoption or not? Did Gemma tell Cindy that I have my
doubts? My eyes meet Emma's. She frowns at me. My eyes
meet Basia's. She tilts her head and looks concerned. Oh, for
God's sake. Is everyone in on this?

"Emma. Why don't you show Cindy your room? Actually,
why don't you show her the whole house?" I suggest. I want to
tell her to show Cindy the entire road, the houses of all the

neighbors, the church, the steeple, anything to get us up and away from the table and the questions.

Gemma and I listen from a room away as Emma guides Cindy through the house. We are curious to find out what Emma deems necessary to tell Cindy. Emma knows that Cindy is a spy from the State Adoption Agency and that she has come to see if our home is a good place for her to grow up. Gemma and I did not want to make too much of her visit, fearing that Emma could become anxious enough to go mute.

"This is where we watch TV and where I play a lot. We call it the Family Room. It's kind of messy."

Perfection. We did not force her to learn any lines. Honest.

"This is where Kiki does her writing. We call it, Kiki's Office, but it has a lot of other stuff in it, too. Kiki doesn't like stuff. We are going to get a new window put in because this one is letting in cold air."

We should get Emma a job as a docent at a museum. Man, is she good. We listen to her finish the tour with a flourish. "And that is our whole house."

Cindy looks at Gemma and me, standing in the dining room, proud and surprised. She raises her eyebrows again, this time with an impressed air, a satisfied, almost triumphant stance. In moments when she can honestly conclude that a child has landed in a world within which she will thrive, Cindy must feel not only relieved, but also, hopeful.

By now, Emma has made her way over to Gemma and me. We put our arms around her, without thinking. Basia wants in on it. She sticks her head directly into the huddle. This is just about as gooey as it can get. I'm not sure I would fall for this if I were Cindy. I'm not so sure I fall for it as Carol. Cindy leaves with a smile on her face.

"I have to come back one more time, just as a formality. You can set up a time to meet with the judge. Congratulations!"

What a world. What a Vermont, is more like it. Here we are, two women in a lesbian relationship, being given the go-ahead to adopt a little girl. The only person who threw out a roadblock was Sam. Nowhere else in the process has anyone said, "But, you're two women. You aren't allowed to adopt a child." So far, no one has counseled us on the possible problems inherent with a same-sex adoption. Even the judge at the anticlimactic seal-of-approval meeting, (which takes all of fifteen minutes), smiles, gushes even, and tells us how lucky we all are as he sends us off into the November sunset.

But, of course, it is not like this everywhere. There are only a handful of states where a same-sex couple can adopt a child without legal hindrances. I am betting that there are only a handful of communities like the one we live in, where the acceptance is heartfelt and exuberant.

There is a community supper held once a month in the basement of the white church which graces the center of our village. It was at the November supper that we "came out" as a real, legal-like family. One hundred people rose to their feet, up from the rickety, wooden chairs and applauded. I had Emma on my shoulders and Gemma by my side. A few people were crying and of these, perhaps two could be counted as intimate friends. Were they crying out of disgust and aversion? I can't be absolutely sure but I'm guessing that these people were crying from a sense of justice and, like Cindy, hope. Here was a child embraced and held up by a community, wishing the best for her and the two people appointed by the fates, to raise her. It not only did not matter that we were two women asked to take Emma on, it counted as a step forward—a look into what a world could be when wisdom, love, and responsibility win out over fear.

In our small community, as insular as it can be at times, many of us are trying to grow up and away from what scares and challenges us. There are no perfect communities. There are no perfect people. But there are moments that come amazingly close to being perfect. Standing in front of our neighbors that night was one of those moments. As with our civil union ceremony held four years previous to our adoption of Emma, this would be one memory sure to provide me with reasons to believe in something better: the struggle and fruition of going beyond our personal needs and fears for the greater good.

The only problem with moments is that they don't last. No kidding. We walked out of the church that night, filled with the possibility of sweet things to come. I tried to hold onto the effects of that moment for as long as I could. But soon enough, I succumbed to a temptation that had been lying dormant inside my cells for fifteen years.

Happy fiftieth birthday, Carol! How about a glass of red wine to go with those age lines?

12
BECOMING FIFTY

*H*appy Birthday, CarolO!

What do you want? To drink without ceasing and here's what I promise you, everyone. That when I drink, I will be thinking of you coming at me from across the room with accusatory glares, sharp and twisted dark eyes that are cursing me in disapproval. I will think of you discovering me, bottle to mouth in a giant moment of slugging back a washing swallow. I will picture you each and every glass full. I will live in the guilt that your image will evoke.

Happy Birthday, CarolO! Fifty years old and drinking again. Here's a toast to your failure. A toast to the madness of the secrets that lash you to the bow of a sinking ship. Some maidenhead: looking straight into the face of the deep, unrelenting sea. Go ahead, take a drink. Fling all reason into the

waves of self-pity and self-martyrdom and rationalization—
these things designed for this only: to convince you that you
deserve a drink after fifteen years of sobriety given everything
you have been through and have been asked to do. Celebrate
the fact that you have stepped up to the plate and done an ad-
mirable job of it. You have successfully been raising Emma.
No kidding. There is no harm in a drink. Italy, here I come.

I am here beneath the wisteria arbor in Niovole, Italy. The
sun in early evening here in Tuscany is like blown-open sea
foam: soft, gauzy, and warm. My father raises a glass of red
wine to the muses of oil painters who surely are flying above
his wavy white hair. My sisters Kate and Michele, my father,
and Jan (my father's companion) lift their glasses for the toast.
I add my glass of water to the undulating swirls of red; it is
lonely here in my glass of water. This does not feel like
strength, wisdom, and clarity, the things they promise in Alcoholics Anonymous. It feels pitiful, like I am being left out of
the celebration my father requested in his return to Italy after
sixty years: a return to where he was stationed during the opening phases of World War II. This time, my father, a fine artist,
wants to be able to paint what he sees, not just watch help-
lessly from the back of an army transport or boat.

But I will not taste the nectar of these celebrations, my father's and my own secret celebration, the one I promised myself just before I boarded the plane. I will be outside the circle.
The injustice of being proclaimed an alcoholic falls all around
me, striking and biting. I cannot thwart this attack—unpre-

pared as I am against my compulsion to drink. I have not felt this in years. There is no reason to hold myself back from succumbing to this urge, not even the promise I made to Gemma that I would not drink in Italy; she will never find out.

And so, it starts. As easily as reaching for the bottle that is less than an arm's length away. I will take just one taste.

The first swallow possesses all the majesty of that first requited kiss. As soon as the rim of the glass is to my mouth, I become an aching, longing lover, who can think of nothing else but having more. My eyes close and I am in a swoon. She has come back to me. I am hers, head over heels, legs, body, and heart, hers. The taste of the wine rests in my mouth as the liquid cascades down my throat. The wine is everywhere now. It is in every sense: I smell, taste, touch, hear, and see only red. Then it moves on into every cell. The glass is back up to my lips. I can have more! I can really have more! I simply cannot believe my good fortune.

Then, I look out at my sisters, my father, and Jan. All of them are watching me expectantly. In an instant, without flinching, I speak the first of many lies: "It's all right. I can drink these days. No problem. I'm just drinking while I'm on this trip. Y'know, to kind of celebrate with you guys."

There's a moment of scrutiny and suspicious consideration, and then acceptance. They do not want to spoil their own moment of bliss and begin, what could turn out to be, a "scene."

"Are you sure, honey?" Jan queries, the bravest, perhaps, and the most objective member of the gang.

"I'm sure, Jan," I state with all the command of a sergeant

about to send her troops into a doomed and ill-conceived battle. If there are any more doubts, no one expresses them and our glasses are raised again, this time with the color red reigning supreme.

Let the celebration begin!

My eyes open first thing in the morning and I am thinking about when I can have the first glass of wine that day without appearing too eager. Obviously breakfast is out. Not even Italians drink at that hour of the day, I think. Lunch? It depends. I could probably get away with one glass, maybe two, but it would be better if I didn't drink until either early or mid-afternoon. I could slip away by myself and drive to a bar (is that what they call them here?) and have a couple of glasses. Or, I could pour myself a glass here at the villa and keep it under wraps. What kind of wraps is the question. By the pool under a towel? In my room behind the books on my nightstand? I could just swig it out of a bottle—that way no one would even know I was slugging. I could wait until we all go out for dinner; I'll insist on an early one and see if someone offers me a glass. I could say "No, thanks," all the while knowing I can have some later back at the villa. That way, the gang will think I don't even give a flying squeak whether I drink or not. That might be the best way to go: feigned indifference.

I am leaning toward the disinterested approach, but by noon, I cannot stand it anymore. I pour myself a glass of wine and go out to the pool for a swim, glass in hand for all to see. No one says a word.

It is a relatively slow ride back to the frontlines, over the following weeks and months, which includes the celebration of my fiftieth birthday two weeks after my return from Italy. The secret sips at my birthday party do not present a problem to my scheming mind. It's, "Ah yes, and away we go." If I am caught, it's a no-brainer response: "Just taking a taste or two tonight." I make sure Gemma is never around when I sneak it. By the time everyone has gathered in the dining room to sing "Happy Birthday" to me, I am comfortably settled into a three-glass state of renewed inebriation. The trick is to appear happy and giddy without appearing sloppy or awkward with exaggerated gestures and half-swallowed phrases. The trick seems to be working.

Oh my God, this feels familiar and the tip of the realization that this is a dangerous familiar feeling begins to appear over the horizon of my now-skewed perspective. As quickly as it rises, it falls back and away, forced out of sight by my remarkably efficient denial skills. I am in it for a long stretch. This night—celebrating fifty years of life—I do not believe there is trouble brewing within my chemically altered body. I am convinced this is a one-night stand and that in the morning, my gorgeous lover will have left, clothes, wallet, and jewelry nowhere to be found. I have discovered a way back to a place where there is no pain, no confusion, and no guilt. I have found a way back to my secret place; it is mine and mine alone. Gemma and Emma cannot find me. No one can.

What happens to us alcoholics when we "slip" is like a betrayal of the deepest sort. Similar to cancerous cells that become voracious in their drive for sustenance and reproduction, the alcoholic system becomes bent on the insane urge for poison. Even as we are raising bottle or glass or needle or pill closer to the entrance, knowing full well what will happen once we let the poison in, messages from our betrayer are being blasted over the cellular intercom. Taunting and slicing through to the very core of our reason, the voices will not be silenced or denied.

Listen to me. Right now, as I sit here writing in the early morning, one hour into this day, I have already thought about having a drink.

Life will present itself to you, CarolO. It will wake you up each morning, rousing you from that maze of pity and force you to see the hummingbird which is sitting on the stem of the coleus that grows in the window box just outside the east-facing window. Life will blow in through the cracks between door and frame. It will scream at you to pay attention. Pay attention! Take that stupid drink out of your hand, CarolO!

I can't.

I won't.

When it gets too hard, when obligations and responsibilities overwhelm you, threatening to bury you alive, reach for a way out. A drink. No one will know.

Gemma and I are driving home. She has been abnormally silent for the past half an hour. The silence is creating a jittery tension in me. I wait for the question that I know has been coming toward me since I came back from Italy. I know that she has smelled alcohol on my breath. I know she has sensed the change in me these last few weeks. The fact that she hasn't said anything or asked anything yet has been odd. She clears her throat.

"Did you drink in Italy?"

"Yes, I did."

Gemma doesn't respond. We drive the rest of the way home in screaming, raging, bellowing silence. She gets out of the car and heads up the stairs without a word or glance in my direction. When I get into the house, she is already on the phone, moving quickly into the bedroom, closing the door, barring me from entering. I can hear her high-pitched voice, mixed with sobs, streaming out from underneath the door. Basia has already disappeared out the front door and down the stairs; she won't return until the tension has dissipated, which, from the sound of it, could be a long time.

I don't know what to do now. I don't know what to do.

Emma, Gemma, and the family we have been trying to become are falling away—down toward the place in me where all failures reside. I did not want this to happen. I wanted to let her in, honest. I wanted to let all of this in. And, in all truth, I thought I had. But the stinging, sinking realization of my resistance cannot be ignored or denied.

Gemma opens the door of our bedroom and, with a swollen, red face, tells me that she wants me to move out. Gemma wants me to leave. I have become more of a burden than an asset. My behavior is tearing holes through the substrata of our lives together. It would be easier for Gemma if I left, that way she would only have Emma to worry about, take care of, and create lists for.

I don't recognize Gemma. I don't recognize myself. I don't know what is in the way anymore. I thought it was grief—the pounding axe of my longing for the lost: my sisters, my mother, my home on the cliffs—people and places ripped from me, leaving sharp-edged blades to do the bloodletting. These are losses I will always be feeling. These are not wounds still waiting to be healed. These are not voids continuing to need filling.

When Emma showed up, I began to feel all this discomfort, all this pain. And now, Gemma and Emma are beginning to fall away for reasons I don't understand. I cannot reach for them because I don't know how to reach out anymore. I cannot reach for them because I don't want to know how. It is too much work.

I ask Gemma to wait before making a final decision. I ask her to remember what we promised each other at our civil union ceremony: to learn from the broken promises and the mistakes, not to go back in time but to be right here together, learning from each other.

And there's more, Gemma. I want to be here without apologies, without excuses, lies, and crumbling alibis. I want a looseness of limbs and heart. I want to savor you, bent over backwards in awe of your features and attributes. I want to love you right now, for who you are right now. Burned. Angry. Lost.

Hurt. Fed-up. This woman tight and overwhelmed. This control freak. This fifty-year-old woman. I want to love you, not the woman I married six years ago. Not the woman I met on the dance floor of a bar on Valentine's Day night sixteen years ago. I want our love to move on from the images we have of each other, the ones that hold us back. I want to find the evolving passion—the place where it is burning now. I want to ride it out beyond this day of broken promises and requests that cut away all hope. I want you to change your mind. I want you to see that I am right here, stepping up to the plate, even if I am not always fully present.

Love fights, Gemma. Love draws up sides and puts us on opposite sides of the fence. It says one thing to you and another thing to me. Love makes us defensive and offensive. It forces us to say things that we will regret forever. Love insists that we grow up. And I am trying to grow up

"I want you to change your mind. I want you to give it a couple of days. OK?" I ask with straight on sincerity.

Gemma listens without moving. Her expression is one of complete contempt. A solid wall of contempt. She will not move. Maybe she will never move again.

"I cannot trust anything you say."

"Yes you can. When I say I love you and Emma, I mean it. There are some things I mean with all my heart."

"You are so full of shit. Why did you drink when you promised me that you wouldn't? Why?"

"Because there was no promise once I was there. I simply

reached out for the bottle of red wine and started drinking. I wasn't thinking about you. I was thinking about that moment and celebrating with my family."

"That's what I mean. You don't care about anyone else when you want something badly enough."

"Do you have any idea how much I think about you and Emma every day? How much I plan around what needs to happen and what I need to do for you every day?"

This blow for blow will end badly. It will not be measured equally. We will both wind up shortchanged. We both want enough. We want someone to tell us that we have given enough, thought enough, planned enough, loved enough for everyone in the world. But that will never happen.

"Stop it! Stop it! I can't listen to you! Go away! Go somewhere, just please, go away from me right now!"

And I do. I go away. But not too far away. Because I know that she needs me. And she always will.

Separation does not necessarily translate into physical distance. I went away from Gemma. I did not move away from our home, but I went away from her, farther than I had ever gone before. The days turned into churning, bubbling baths of toxic gases. Neither one of us can breathe here in the rooms we inhabit; the air growing thicker and more dense by the minute. We do not reach out for each other here, in this poisonous environment we have created. I sleep in the living room, crawling into a sleeping bag, cocooning myself away from Gemma. It is the end of September, still warm out, but

I am cold at night, so cold without Gemma sleeping next to me.

I hate putting Emma to bed now. Every other night, it is still my responsibility to read and comfort her until she falls asleep. I wait until the very last minute to enter her bedroom, filled with the kind of resentment that plagued our first nights together, three years ago. This time, my resentment feels lethal. I want to blame Emma, again, hold her responsible for the smashed and broken state of my marriage. I want to shout out over the sweet little book we are reading that I'm done with this charade, this insincere farce we are performing in. All on our best behavior? Going on as if nothing was wrong? I never wanted this. Never. I wanted Gemma and Basia and me to have a simple life, coming toward truths and consequences in our own time. And now, that simple life is gone, never to be retrieved again. Slowly, I am forgetting everything I once needed to know about my marriage to make it work for both of us. I am forgetting who I married and why. I am sinking further into my desire to drink, forgetting why I stopped drinking in the first place. I walk out into each day, as if in a trance, motivated only by the improbable possibility that my life with Gemma will come back to me, that we will recognize each other again. That I will remember what it is I forgot.

What I Forgot

Today, at about 5 o'clock,
I forgot how much I owed you.
I forgot that there was an old dog waiting outside

on the front porch,
and that she was dying.

I forgot that I had to behave myself
for everyone who loves me.
I forgot that the mud is deep and cannot be driven through
with a Toyota Matrix,
so low to the ground.

There is this forgetting,
and there is that forgetting.
Either way, it only last as long as it takes to write it down.

I forgot that wet wood does not catch fire.

I forgot that we are in trouble.

You and me.

We are in trouble.

That's what I forgot.

13
CALL ME "GRANDPA"

*W*hat mischievous and diabolical force brings us together and turns us into families? The most unlikely of familial combinations rise up out of the riot of romantic love. Once the relationship is more established and we meet the "folks" and extended kin, we look across at each other at some dinner table, trying to make sense of it all. Who the blink *are* these people anyway? How did they get in here? Who let them in? Then come the added attractions such as: the grand kids, the nieces, the nephews, and the in-laws. We look at our partners wondering if there has been some grave mistake. "Are you certain that this is your family, sweetheart?" But then, of course, it turns out to be true and the resemblances start becoming more and more obvious, much to our absolute horror and, I suppose, at times, to our delight.

No one escapes this fate, as far as I can tell. I have never met anyone who got away with immunity from the trials and tribulations of dealing with family. And there is no award given for having the most dysfunctional kinfolk. The only prize comes with awareness that it wouldn't be much different around the block at someone else's house. Look in through any picture window and a familiar scene will greet you.

Families, in varying forms of coming to know each other, getting in as close as they can, must arrive at ways of making room without blowing their covers, blowing each other away, or blowing it altogether. A balancing act is required, the acquisition of which can be tedious and, sometimes, impossible to maintain. That is why we must have survival tactics, especially at the formal gatherings where best behavior is supposed to rule with agreed upon manners the operative physical means used to achieve that end.

There are roles each one of us takes on, filling niches created by the family dynamics. If there is not a family clown, for instance, or if the anointed family clown is a dud or worse yet, inappropriate, then that role can be assumed by the new lover of one of the family members. This role is a much coveted one, I have discovered, always being in the running for the role of family clown. I have witnessed people fighting over the role of family clown in subtle and not so subtle ways.

The family clown must, at every family event, ease the tension that will eventually creep in, even when everyone seems to be following the unspoken rules of decorum. The family clown has to be vigilant, always gauging the tone of the interactions so that, when the inevitable gaffe or deadly lull occurs, she or he can slip in with just the right story, joke, face, irreverent remark, political dig (tricky and a bit risky), or even a slapstick-like physical blunder. This isn't easy, especially if the crowd is of mixed age. No family clown wants to scare a child or say something so off-color that it causes the parents of the child or children to get up and leave, offspring in tow. That kind of faux pas can put a temporary stop to the event. The family members, with glaring looks of dissatisfaction flying directly at the family clown, disbands and retreats to the far corners of the house to analyze and trash the clown's rude behavior. Sometimes, this kind of discharging, aimed at an obvious scapegoat, helps to diffuse the tension, bringing back a necessary equilibrium and the family can come back together for more.

There can be more than one family clown just as there can be more than one whiner, bastard, party-pooper, or "special" cousin, (the one everyone whispers about behind closed doors). If the newcomer is to become integrated into the configuration which has already been established, no matter what role he or she assumes, there must be a gracious entry—a subtle slipping in so everyone can get used to the change that the fresh energy brings to the table.

Just as the introductions of adults into families shifts the pulse of power, so does the introduction of a new child, baby or older. There we were, Gemma and I, sitting comfortably established at our dinner table at night, Basia quietly making her begging presence known, when Emma came to dinner to stay. Gone were the days of conversations that lasted for the duration of the meal. Gone were evenings of retelling the day's events sensitively evoked by the caring partner. Also gone were the teasing, the sexual innuendo, the arguing, the prying, and the talking about Tanya and Emma. Dramatic and instant, the family dynamic spun three hundred and sixty degrees around and back again — the final result was a completely different mix.

Emma and I are both family clowns — we like the attention and we like making people laugh. This is fine most nights, when a balance can be reached and Gemma isn't turned into the third wheel, looking us with impatient disdain. The three of us also have to be careful not to let Emma float up and away, pulling all the focus with her and transforming dinner into the Emma Comedy Hour or Emma's Masterpiece Dinner Theater. If given half a chance, Emma will take the attention and not let it go. At the larger gatherings, especially at the ones where Emma's presence did not pose any challenges because she simply was not there, the world has altered significantly. Take the unfaltering adoring aunt attention away from nieces and one nephew and watch the fireworks begin. For the opening ten years of my niece, Anna, and my nephew, Paul, I played a major part — Bub to Anna and Honey Lamby Pie to Paul. They counted on my fully present, one-on-one participation whenever we were together. I could always be counted on to take them on some wild adventure without distractions.

At one of the earlier visits in the Emma-is-with-ustimeline, the tears and harsh words flew. Defenses were raised. Bad behavior rose up without warning. This was a reality no one wanted to face head-on. We tried to let everything slide by, but it didn't work.

One night, I overheard Anna, Paul, and Kate talking. I listened as Anna cried, complaining that Emma was being allowed to get away with selfish and nasty behavior because Anna wanted to go to a movie with me and couldn't; Emma needed me to stay with her. I heard Kate try and explain that Emma was my responsibility now and that I had to be loyal to her. It was clear that at that moment, Anna would not be able to understand and be empathetic; she wanted her Auntie Carol, her Bub, back.

I wish that I had listened silently, taken in the sadness that Anna was expressing and slipped away, leaving her to her feelings without my interference. Caught off-guard, tired, and overwhelmed with the changes my life had already been through, I became angry. Instead of leaving them alone, I made a dramatic entrance, the words not chosen with care and diplomacy.

"Thanks for the education. This has been really important for me to hear," I said with an air of self-righteous indignation as I turned to walk upstairs to bed.

I could hear Anna sobbing, probably more from the shock of my surprise entrance than from the fact that I had overheard her incriminating tirade. But I could not let the night end this way, so I returned and apologized, trying to give Anna not only words that would paint a clear picture of how difficult this was for me but also try to reassure her that she would always be my main Bub—that would never change.

We got through those initial months of discomfort. With time came maturation and an appreciation of what we all needed to do to make our new relationships work.

With my other two nieces, Sarah and Isabelle, my sister Michele's girls, years younger when Emma arrived, Emma has created a connection between our two families that wasn't there before. I was not that close to Sarah and Isabelle when they were babies, unlike my relationships with Anna and Paul. Emma and Sarah are only six months apart in age with Isabelle four years younger. When we all get together, Emma takes off with them and the cousin party begins. I'm guessing and I'm hoping that those relationships will continue to grow, leading all of us toward each other, instead of further away.

I waited until Gemma and I were absolutely sure before making any announcements about adoption possibilities, not wanting to confuse anyone or set up false expectations. I was certain my sisters and my father would have no problem with the news.

"Do you have a picture of her?" my father wanted to know after I first told him about our plan to adopt Emma.

"Sure, Dad. Do you want me to send a copy?"

"Well, yeah! How old is the little girl now?"

"She'll be eight soon. In October, just before the adoption takes place."

"Gee whiz, Carol, dear. This is so very kind of you and Gemma to do this for the little child. How's Gemma's family taking it?"

"Fine, I guess."

"How's the mother of the little girl?"

"Tanya? She's out of the country, Dad. On some island in the Caribbean."

"No kidding!"

I know that my father's capacity to hold two-way conversations is limited so I try to get in as many important details as quickly as I can. He's got a great memory for dates and historical facts but names, not much. I'm never exactly sure how he remembers so many points of reference because he gives the impression of not really listening. I have to shake my head in wonder when he repeats back something I said which I thought for sure he didn't pick up. Conversely, he seems to forget other things such as Emma's name, calling her "the little girl" until I correct him.

When I was a little girl (fortunately, he did remember my name rather often), Dad would call all my girlfriends the same name to their faces. "Genevieve" was his name of choice. Coming home with a friend after school, Sandra C. for example, would usually prove embarrassing if my father was home and if he graced us with his presence, coming in from his studio with a sweep of his hat and smelling like oil paint. "Genevieve! Genevieve! From where the winds blaze a trail across rock and vine! Greetings!" I would glare at him as piercingly direct as possible, never to get through to him. Dad was never great at picking up on the nuances of social communication cues, at least not with my sisters and me. But he can artistically size up a person's facial features within seconds,

rendering a likeness of physical characteristics and temper-
ament that is astonishing. The brilliance of his ability to read
expressions on people's faces and then translate them onto
canvas or paper, has always impressed and baffled me. Interpreting faces for social cues and interpreting them for expressions to be represented in oil paint, watercolor, pencil, or ink,
must happen in different parts of the brain that might be
linked but that are not in the same sphere of comprehension
and execution. But ultimately, it doesn't matter where in his
brain my father's responses and habits originate. He will always be able to charm and impress people with his talent and
his zany antics. My childhood friends were invariably convinced that he was the coolest, if not the wackiest, dad they
knew. I had to agree with "wacky."

By now, fifty years onto a relationship with him, I have
come to know that my father is, indeed, wacky, sometimes
driving those of us who adore him to a point of complete exasperation. By now, I also have come to know that he is the
dearest man on the face of this earth. I forgive him his wackiness not only because its origins are kind, but also because his
wackiness lives in me. My father and I share the zany gene
and the recognition of this fact has brought us closer. When
we speak, mostly by phone these days, I flip instantly into his
world of inane and we soar around together, understanding
everything the other is communicating. Songs, noises, sayings,
quotes, dates, events, names, and places. I understand him
through and through.

This has not gone unnoticed by Gemma, who listens to

my side of the conversations with my father. As I walk around the house with the remote phone planted against my head, talking with my dad, Gemma smiles from the places where our paths intersect. Once off the phone, she will usually shake her head with a short remark to follow like: "It's scary." I don't need to ask what she means by this or other quips. I already know.

"You are so much like your father. It's scary," she has stated on many an occasion, after a phone call, a visit, or after I have made a facial expression that has reminded her of my dad.

"Well, the good news is, he's not a bad man and he's fairly good-looking," I have replied.

"I know that. And yeah, you're right. He's a good man and good-looking, too, but I'm just afraid it's going to look very different on you than it does on him as you get older. I mean, he's got a pretty big nose."

"There are worse things than a big nose."

"I don't think so."

"Oh, c'mon, Gemma. You love my nose."

"I do?"

I run after her, grab her, and stick my nose in her face. She kisses it a dozen times. After that, she has to admit that my nose is perfect, especially perfect because it belongs on my face.

My father's nose is big; so is his heart. The Christmas after we adopted Emma, which was a mere month before, he sent her a Christmas card, as he does for his other four grandchildren.

Inside was a check, made out for the same amount that he gives each of them. Although the printed words were nothing to take special notice of, his sign-off was. With his flamboyant curling letters and bold exclamation marks after practically every word, he wrote the following:

"Merry Christmas, Emma. LOVE, PDO! You can call me Grandpa. God Bless." From then on, the cards have been steady, arriving for her birthday and holidays at least a week in advance of the occasion itself. When he calls or when I call him, I sometimes put Emma on. She does what most kids do when speaking with adults on the phone; she answers in a monotone, "Yes." "Yes," as he asks questions from his end. She smiles and looks at me, waiting for a signal which would permit her to beg off. But on more than one occasion, as she has gotten older, she has actually talked with him past the point when I would normally give the sign-off nod. She always ends the conversation with, "I love you, Grandpa." Because of who my father is, I would have expected nothing less than his acceptance of Emma into the fold of our family, close or extended. He was even welcoming to Gemma once he found out I was in love with her and that "partner" did not mean "business partner" but "life partner."

Letting the rest of my father's family, brothers and sisters, and their offspring, in on my lesbian relationship was beyond tricky; it was a given that I would make no announcements, send out no invitation to our civil union ceremony and never bring Gemma to one of our family reunions. My aunts, uncles, and cousins are all from the conservative Christian side of the tracks, where relationships such as mine are condemned as aberrations and we, the sorry sinning sots, who have succumbed to the devil's influence, need to be prayed for so at least we stand some chance of redemption when the rapture happens. These are good people. They are kind, going out of their way to good deed it through life. They just don't know how to deal with people, particularly family, who have "strayed" from the path set by their god. They pray for me because they don't want me to go to hell with all the other sinners. I don't have the heart or the gall to inform them that hell is where I would rather go because that is where I will hopefully find my sisters, Shari and Danielle (gone to hell for not accepting Jesus before their young and untimely deaths), and other people whom I have loved along the way, sinners one and all.

Over the years as my father's generation has aged and my generation has begun taking the lead, the reunions have taken on a new, more liberal tone. The younger Christians, my cousins, especially a particular trio of sisters and another female cousin I grew up near, have insisted on supporting and loving me for who I am but also opening themselves to Gemma, inviting her to meet the family. Their motives appear to be pure. They want to know Gemma. They want to acknowledge and accept our relationship as a valid expression of love, not condemn it as wrong and immoral. On their insistent and consistent invitations, I finally brought Gemma to a reunion, a few years before we adopted Emma. I guess we figured it was time. The Christian welcome mat was rolled out. Christian good behavior reigned supreme. Best behavior? Absolutely.

I briefed Gemma during our eight-hour drive as to what she could expect. Polite would be the operative baseline for all interactions. There might be moments of ice when judgment would escape from behind the Christian veneer. There would be warm and genuine attempts at conversation that went further than the incidentals. But who knew? Maybe we would all be surprised.

I can always count on Gemma to be charming, appropriate, and helpful. She jumps in whenever and wherever she is needed from helping set up a meal to tearing it down. Gemma knows how to ingratiate herself into the coldest of hearts and situations. Out of all the kinfolk whom Gemma met at that single reunion she attended, only one of my aunts turned her back on her. I will never know why my aunt walked away from Gemma when she was offering out a hand in farewell and I will never ask, but Gemma has no desire to attend another of my family reunions.

The addition of Emma has pushed the door into our lives open a little bit further. My Christian relatives are more willing to look into this den of sin, more willing to care, more interested in asking honest questions about how things are going and, perhaps, more willing to set their judgments aside about my lifestyle choice. There is less focus on the sinning and more on the loving. I never realized before adopting Emma how much having a child can break the long-practiced patterns of communication that either keeps families stuck or estranged. Immediately there is a safe and common ground to step out on. Everyone feels comfortable asking about the kids. In this realm, unless the child is behaving in a particularly bizarre way (cross-dressing, setting cats on fire, piercing unmentionable body parts), questions and ensuing discussions can stay in a zone of the benign. Similar to weather as a topic of conversation, the subject of "the children" or "the child" is easy, simple, and predictable. Emma has steered us into this safe harbor, creating connections that did not exist before.

When I speak with my sisters Michele and Kate, now, we can commiserate about the kids. I have been elevated to a position of parent. I am no longer a bystander who was rarely asked for advice and often left out of a most intimate circle. For the most part, I never minded the distance from the muck and mire of parenthood. Similar to feelings of superiority when Gemma and I were childless, I felt smug listening to parents go on and on about their kids. Teacher workshops, always replete with dutiful and pious parent types, would inevitably turn into bragging festivals about the offspring of all participants. During lunch or ride-sharing, the pictures would be brought out and the stories would begin. Invariably, I would sit quietly, nodding my head, smiling, looking adoringly at supplied photographs and contributing little to the conversations unless a tangent could be sensed and culled from the morass. On the rare occasion when I dared venture down a risky and different path of exploration, such as the time I asked a bunch of women if I should come out to my fifth and sixth grade students, a stunned silence would ensue and

the subject would quickly be brought back to the safe, familiar, and narrow. Ah children! Can we just stick to talking about
the children? All right, all right. Fine.

And now, I can count myself among the kid photograph-
toting masses, whipping out the wallet-size school photo of
Emma when picture sharing time rolls around. I have come
to take pride in showing photos of Emma, not simply because
she is a beautiful child but because it says a heap about where
my priorities are these days. Photographs of kids are like
badges of honor—like medals handed out to those soldiers
who have fought valiantly in battle. Parents do not get badges
to wear on their sleeves or lapels. Parents have their children's
photographs—these are acceptable symbols of our dedica-
tion—the selfless act of raising children. If some nut case ever
pulled out their child's report card or diploma, I'd probably
suggest that they join a Co-dependents Anonymous Group.
But photos, now there's the ticket in.

As much as Emma's presence in our lives has shoved Gemma
and me every which way, including loose, her existence has
brought Gemma closer to her parents, Kay and Don. Here
again, like a Venn diagram, the circles of interest form a large
center of shared concern and devotion. All differences can be
set way outside the parameters of acceptable family behavior.
When Emma enters a room or a conversation, this clan of Italian, French, and Scottish descendants, creates the widest berth
possible to make room for the purest of intentions and the
most open of minds. Although Kay and Don had accepted our

relationship over the twelve years we were together before Emma, there still existed, what I consider to be, a lack of respect. Somehow, our lives were not as valid, not only because we were in a lesbian relationship, but also because we had no children. Of course, both Kay and Don would prefer that Emma remain with Tanya, her rightful mother, but as the deep acceptance of the reality has set in and grown, so have their respect, admiration, and presence. They are regular guests at our dinner table now, many of our evenings spent ohing and ahing over the fabulous meals Gemma creates. Emma is Don's Ootie-Pootie, his affection and adoration of her softening and reshaping every one of his rough edges. He has become a kinder man.

In the "old" days, Don's countenance of hostility and foreboding kept people, particularly his wife and kids, at more than an arm's length away and in a state of constant alert. Don's modus operandi, vigilant to the extreme, determined the mood and atmosphere of every gathering and encounter. I used to dread their visits, anticipating the worst which usually meant showdowns between him and Gemma. Although Gemma's siblings can stand up to Don, she is the only one capable of seeing the confrontations clear through to an end that does not slide down into a surrender. I have witnessed them going head to head, standing back in awe of their full-throttle shouting matches. Since these types of fights never occurred in the home where I grew up with my sisters and father, there is a level of terror that I reach when I'm around for one. When it happens, I either have to leave the house or huddle up with Kay, who, by now, has become accustomed to these displays of fire and will. As I cower, Kay goes on with her routine which may include reading or cooking for everyone, a skill she is an ace at and a skill which takes her away from the front lines. She rarely gets rattled by the fights and when they are over, life continues almost as if nothing happened at all.

The days of Don's eruptive temper are gone now. I sometimes do not recognize the man I met fourteen years ago. I have actually seen love change the shape and features of a man we had all given up as a lost cause. Emma, a healer, without knowing it, has found a way to soothe the beast.

Emma has inadvertently become a bridge, encouraging each one of us to cross over some treacherous-looking rapids. On this we can all agree: Emma's welfare and happiness must come first. In this new land, here on the other side of that bridge, we are asked to become better people. Here in the middle of converging circles, we must stop focusing on all the things that make us different from one another, focusing, instead, on a shared view of the world. Very often, it is a view seen through the eyes of a child and sometimes it is even a view seen through the eyes of a dog, a very concerned dog.

14
AND A DOG
SHALL LEAD THEM

*S*he's a black Lab/Australian sheepdog mix, or so we surmised during the first week of examination and contemplation. The Black Lab we're sure of, the Australian Sheepdog not so. The small triangular ears that flap continually whenever she trots or runs (which she doesn't do much anymore) lead us to think that there is either Collie or Sheepdog in her. And the fact that she herds or used to.

In her day, slim and frisky, Basia would tear across the ground, in swirling circles, tucking in her tail and using her rear end to "herd." Not that there was anything for her to herd. We never possessed sheep, goats, or cows. She would try to herd us, a toddling Emma mostly. We came to call this obvious genetic dance of hers, "Mad Dog." Whenever she broke into it, one of us would shout, "She's doing Mad Dog!"

Around and around she would go, seemingly roused by an emotion we could only guess at. I would like to believe it was euphoria; so taken with a feeling of divine bliss, she could do only one thing: herd and herd madly.

She doesn't do Mad Dog much anymore. The last time she tried, her back legs gave out and she wound up collapsed and rolling like a large sausage down our sloping lawn. These episodes are traumatic for all of us. If it seems that she might be getting ready to do Mad Dog these days, we stop her, fearing what could follow: hours of limping and moaning. We attempt to comfort her if she seems to be in pain, but Basia doesn't like our concerned attention. She only asks for our affection when she is feeling good or needs something like a walk first thing in the morning, and I mean, First Thing in the Morning. The past few weeks, Basia has been getting me up at 5:30 a.m., just when the light and the birds begin their opening music. Basia clicks into our room, toenails tapping out her arrival on my side of the bed, and she stands there, her heavy breathing waking me from the deepest of slumbers.

"OK, Twirly. I'm up. Let's go."

There are mornings when annoyance fills my greetings, but mostly I give her the best of my words at first light. After I massage her face, we step out onto the porch together, each of us inhaling deeply and listening intently as we survey the garden and woods beyond. I'm sure that I can hear more than she can: the sound of the waterfall down slope, the phoebe calling from across the creek, and the sheep bleating from the neighbor's house half a mile up. I'm sure she can smell more than I can, holding up that large snout of hers into the breeze-borne stream of information full of the previous nights' animal trespassers. I can smell roses, the small, wild pink ones that grace the borders of our property and everyone else's property along the back roads in Vermont. I can smell hints of cold grass that by midday, with the sun so strong and high, will be a riotous waft of steamed plant ingredients: the lawn becoming a veritable stovetop of cooking chlorophyll. But I know Basia smells much more than this and more deeply.

I'm not so certain about Basia's eyesight, but from the appearance of her eyes, cloudy and out of focus much of the time, I'm betting she cannot see worth beans. These days I use large, dramatic arm signals to direct her. She stands immobilized by her growing sense of insecurity at the threshold of our porch and so I must wave with my big white shirt on, first to get her attention, then to indicate where I want her to go: "To the yard, Basia. You haven't peed in hours. C'mon, Twirly. I'll help you." I speak to her even though she can't hear me. The words I speak and the way I speak them is meant to comfort me, not to help her.

Some mornings Basia is brave or perhaps more desperate to get on with her morning routine. She steps right out onto the porch without any coercion or coaxing. Her ears are perky, her tail, too. Everything about her says, "I'm ready for this day." She stumbles down the stairs with a purpose, one seemingly beyond the need to urinate, looking around as if anticipating the presence of a dog that needs to be scared away from her domain or a chipmunk that is being too rowdy and needs some discipline. She's back to being the "Concerned Citizen," a name my father gave her a few years back on one of his rare visits. For Basia is concerned—her entire demeanor has always been one of concern. At least it is the emotional state we have ascribed to her expressions and countenance. Basia has the appearance of one who is actively listening, like she is ready to hear confessions and worries.

One day, not long ago, I returned home after a particularly grueling day at work, feeling as lost as a navigator without constellations to chart a course by. I was overwhelmed with my job as head teacher of a program for adolescents with autism, recently coming to the sobering realization that ninety percent of the job was administrative, not a skill I can claim to be good at nor have much interest in becoming good at. I wasn't getting to teach much, which is a skill I possess in great measure and love doing. Add to this sense of dread the growing feeling of inadequacy that I was beginning to feel at home. I wasn't doing a very good job of being a parent or a partner. There was judgment at every turn, with eyes scrutinizing my every action: there was no way to rise to the tasks set before me.

On this day—particularly ripe with obsessive thoughts about my inadequacies as a special education teacher, parent, and partner—I walked into our house in a state of total droop. Basia was not there to greet me with her usual display of enthusiasm. I found her in our bedroom, deeply asleep on her dog bed. I sat down on the floor next to her, as she popped up, surprised and then, disoriented. When she fully realized it was me, she let out a huge sigh—it sounded like relief. Her ears were sticking straight out to the sides of her head—my sleepy old dog. As soon as I touched her flank, the tears started. I didn't have to think about it—there were no images to conjure, no words of chastisement to draw upon, no Celtic melody to hum softly to make myself cry. These tears were direct from the no-fly zone. Controlling or stopping them was clearly not an option. I gave in to them.

Basia looked at me with her tilted head of concern. I thought for sure that she would get up and head for the door, made uncomfortable by my crying. She continued to lie there with the kindest eyes. Then she began to lick my salty hand— the one I was using to wipe away the tears. Her simple act of, what I took to be compassion, threw me further into sobs.

"Twirly, you're the only one who understands." Basia stood up and began licking my face, something she was not in the habit of doing. Her tongue, lamb's ear soft, cleaned every inch of my face. I did not try to push her away—why would I? At one point, she licked one of my eyes just as a tear escaped from the corner. She smacked her lips as if testing it for salt content. I began to laugh, grabbing her head with both my hands and kissing her all over her face and snout. She pulled back, wagging her tail and giving me the tilted-head once over.

"You ready for a walk, Twirly?"

We raced to the door with Basia winning by a nose. Once down the stairs, she dashed across the yard to find a suitable place to pee, being particular when it comes to choosing the perfect spots. She was so excited that I thought she might attempt "Mad Dog," so I ran to her. My unusual behavior caused her to become even more riled up and, sure enough, she sped off into "Mad Dog." I was too late to stop her, so I clapped instead. She made it around the yard once more before her back legs quit. The collapse wasn't as bad as her collapses could be. I got to her in time to help her stand again. I brushed her off and we headed for the road; we both seemed to know what should come next: a short afternoon constitutional. I wished that I had a tail then, too. I wanted us to be two happy dogs walking side by side down a dirt road en route to our favorite stream where we would dunk, drink, and shake together. I wanted to wag with her.

But after a few minutes of walking side by side, woman and dog, I was glad to be her human companion. I loved how she kept looking back at me as we walked, checking to make sure that I was there and that I was all right. I smiled every time she turned to look at me. It was a smile as genuine and full of thanks as it could possibly be and I was absolutely certain that she understood.

Gemma and I are sitting on the living room couch; trying not to let this argument get out of control but if she calls me lazy, selfish, or boneheaded one more time, then out of control we will be. Gemma is too close—with her dangerously wide eyes; I want to put two black eye patches on her, rendering her blind and ineffective as an accuser. She finds the stinging words with precision—the path from emotion to language and back to mouth/eyes must be a short one for her with no obstacles along the way.

I'm in bumbling, drooling idiot mode—everything coming out sounding like an attempt at covering my butt. Gemma's eyes and acerbic slings have, once again, rendered me in a state of confusion. I cannot remember what is true or not; it all sounds plausible.

"I thought I had enough money in my bank account for the drainage."

"And it mysteriously disappeared? I want to know what you spent it on."

"Right now?"

"Yes. Right now. Tell me."

"I don't remember exactly. Sneakers. Newspapers. The kids. Gas."

"All right. Stop. This is obviously bullshit. You couldn't possibly have spent that much on sneakers. How do you expect me to trust you, Carol? How?"

I'm stumped.

"You can't answer me because you don't know the answer because you're lying to me."

"I'm not lying. I'm confused."

"I'll bet you're confused."

By now, our voices have reached the higher ranges—we're both beginning to sound like insane macaws. Whatever self-monitoring skills we were in possession of half an hour previous, the surge of adrenaline coursing through our blood is zipping right past STOP, heading full speed ahead, to GO. We cannot be thwarted. We must fight. That is, until Basia enters the room, stage left.

At first, we take no notice of her as she slinks into the room, head, ears, and tail tucked below her body. She is as inconspicuous as a shadow. We cannot hear the clicking of her long toenails because here in the living room the wooden floor is rugged. She is panting, barely. Out of the far corners of my eyes, I see her moving back and forth in front of the couch, occasionally brushing up against our legs. Gemma and I continue to rage but already some of the venom has been extricated. Basia's presence has subconsciously made us tone it down a notch or two, but we slug on.

Basia will have none of it. She has come into the living room to do one thing: end the fight. As quietly and stealthily as a trained counselor, she raises her front legs onto the couch between us and forcefully places her nose an inch in front of Gemma's mouth, almost in it. Effective tactic?

Gemma is cut off mid-sentence. I am cut off mid-retort. In an instant our hearts burst open, shame and remorse filling the cracks. I don't know whether to cry or laugh and ultimately it doesn't matter what happens now. The fight is over. Gemma and I have no choice but to end it and move on, but not before we shower all manner of affection on Basia for leading us out of this latest mutual assault.

"Our little mediator," Gemma says, tears beginning at the rims of her normal-sized eyes.

I'm sorry, Basia. I'm so sorry.

The hole is dug. The major mound of dirt is looming on the hill at the back of our house above the stream. The veterinarian has been summoned. Basia is to be euthanized on Saturday morning.

There is no preparing for this. I can't see straight. I'm not sure how to get to school each day, familiar directions and givens all seem strange. The intercostal muscles ache as if I have been punched in the ribs by a heavyweight boxer or taken a fall off a cliff. I can't catch my breath.

Basia wanders, her toe nails clicking out the beat of her own funeral march. She doesn't seem to know us, barking at me in the middle of the night, sniffing us as if we are foreigners to these parts. We find her urine everywhere by stepping in it, unprepared in socks or bare feet. She is not happy. She is crying. She is moaning.

Friday comes. Basia is up and at the door before the sun breaks. Her tail is up, the film drawn back from her eyes. She can't wait to eat, attacking the chicken broth and kibble as if tasting it for the first time. Basia is back.

Six months on. The hole is still dug and looming. Maybe Basia knows it's there and what it is waiting for. Maybe we need her to be here with us just a little bit longer, leading us toward truths we are incapable of finding on our own. Maybe she has a good life. Maybe this is her place, here with us, this mottled family of sensitive gals.

She breathes loudly in the next room. I count on this rhythm and I will continue to for as long as she lives. I will keep my voice lowered. I will walk the yard each morning, gathering up her poop and sending it over the bank. I will wash and tend the wound on her back. I will mark my steps with an awareness of impermanence. I will try to remember all of these things as I cherish our brave old dog—Basia, the Twirly Girl, my Sugar Drop.

15
AT THE FOOT
OF HER BED

I am standing at the foot of Emma's bed; she isn't in it because she is spending five days with Tanya. The blankets, sheets, pillows, stuffed animals, used tissues, underwear, pajamas, hair-ties, dolls, doll clothes, and magazines are haphazardly strewn as if Emma threw them in the air all at once, not waiting to see how they would land or where they would land. Her bed is the zone of chaos—Emma can turn her bed into this kind of frenetic art installation in a matter of minutes. There are certain times of day and night when her creative brilliance is at its peak. Frequently, these spurts start at night, as she sleeps.

Emma enters a well-made bed between the hours of seven and nine, optimally. We try to get her into her room for the wind down on school nights early because on school nights she is always revved up—filled with all the words and images she spent the majority of her energy trying to interpret and respond to during the day. Mostly, Emma works things out through playing with her dolls. Gemma and I can hear her, giving voice to her Barbies, Polly Pockets, or American Girl dolls in her room or the family room. She has a lot of dolls, none of which were purchased by me. I can spend money with the best of them, but I rarely give into pressure from Emma or culturally induced guilt to buy her stuff she wants or, more often, doesn't want. She has more than enough people who spoil her with gifts, which in my opinion, are meaningless and, worse still, harmful because the endless procurement of needless junk encourages addiction: that ache for wanting more. I stand at the foot of Emma's bed, surveying the landscape of the room Gemma and I have helped her put together. I often wish she didn't have so much junk, for junk is certainly what most of her room is home to. I have gone so far as to remove things from her room without telling her or Gemma; neither one has ever noticed the missing fodder. Hah!

But tonight I am not standing at the foot of Emma's bed in judgment or condemnation of her material possessions or of anything else I might find suspect or distasteful. I am standing at the foot of Emma's bed, missing her, wanting this bed to be rocking with her presence—the shape and size and motion of her body flinging everything in her path to the far reaches of her bed and beyond. I stand here in awe of the mess she has made, in awe of the places things wind up, amazed that a pair of sneakers could land so far apart, in almost different hemispheres. I am in awe of how she inhabits her room, our house, and the realms that stretch out toward places she is discovering.

For Emma, there is not a whole lot of rest in between adventures. She slips into her bed, blankets turned down for her entrance each night by Gemma or me. As soon as her legs sink into the sheets, they are moving; she is not able to stop them at first. Her feet keep moving until exhaustion demands that they cease. There is a palpable end to this fidgeting—like the balloon has finally given up its last burst of air. There is a sputter—a last rising up of legs, arms, and voice—and then either a flat-line silence or a slight intake or outtake of breath before a release and a wave of peace. Since I don't sleep with Emma, it's hard to know when her legs start moving again. After she has fallen asleep, she is motionless, her breath a stilled hush. But at some point in the night, motion begins again, for by morning, her bed is a heap, a crosscurrent of all things made of fabric and her body is turned in a direction defying the laws of physics and human anatomy.

We have found her turned upside down, head against the bottom white-painted wooden slats, hands clutching them tightly in her small fists. We have found her with legs sticking straight out into the void of her room. How she could get into and remain in this position without falling onto the floor or waking up is a question that will probably never be sufficiently answered unless we set up a video camera and capture her twisting and turning on film.

The fact is: Emma must move. She was given this genetic

propensity by her parents. It is up to Gemma, myself, and everyone else who instructs or cares for her to make sure she has plenty of room to move and that she is safe as she moves. I take her to the woods. I take her to the fields. I take her to the hills, the streams, and the pools fed by rock-splashed waterfalls.

Emma and I share the traits of the restlessly excited, but I have had many more years of flailing—my cells are tired, sometimes so exhausted that they refuse to be roused. I can do only one thing when I am that spent: plunge, backside down first, onto a couch, bed, or ground and lie completely still, staring. I stare at a wall, ceiling, or sky, my awareness floating beyond the reach of conscious thought. Gemma will ask, "What are you doing?" By the look of me, I would've thought it was pretty obvious, but I reply anyway, "Nothing." This baffles Gemma. A state of nothingness is an impossibility to her. Gemma is always in the process of doing or planning for the doing. The guilt that I used to experience whenever I allowed myself these moments of nothing no longer exists. I know enough about myself now to silently insist on these breaks in the action of my body and mind and if Gemma gets upset or questions the purpose of such respites, she doesn't let on. Wisely and compassionately, she leaves me to my nothing.

Emma is in a squeaky mood. At morning light, a Saturday, with no buses to catch or cars to get ready for, she sleepily and slowly shuffles to where I am creating my morning cup of coffee/sludge. She looks up at me and reaches her arms above her head. I bend over and scoop her up, all sixty-four pounds of her. How can it be that she feels lighter than she did a few days ago? Her arms are around my neck, her legs around my waist. I hold her close with my arms, chin, and heart. I don't want her to move. She smells so good and she is holding so still, every bit of her so close and warm. Right now her heartbeat is a butterfly wing against my chest and similar to the emergence of a Monarch from its casing, Emma is beginning to wake up, energy radiating out into her limbs. It is the reverse of her before-bed process. Gradually she is coming alive and I know within the next ten minutes or so, she will be at full steam and we will have to step back and watch her race off into the day. I close my eyes. I am thinking: "Stay still. Stay still here. Just a few more seconds, Emma." Once I let her go, setting her feet down onto the tiles of our kitchen, Emma will be in her flurry, until the night welcomes her back into its hold. We can't catch her nor can we slow her down. We can just try to give her room and help her with the inevitable bumps and bruises that come with being so alive.

I am sitting at the foot of Emma's bed now. She is still gone, halfway through the five days she is spending with Tanya. I was able to set her loose into her mother's arms this time, without the usual scowl and perfunctory nod of the head. I was even able to stand on the porch and watch them drive off, waving like I really meant them the best trip ever. Basia, Gemma, and I went back into the house and stood in the dining room, looking at each other expectantly. Basia's eyes moved back and forth between my face and Gemma's face, waiting for one of us to say something or make a move.

"OK, Pack Leader, what do we do now?" Gemma asked, for over the years I have become the Pack Leader to Basia and I have a responsibility to determine the next step. It's great to have at least one member of our family who thinks that I am in charge. I held my hands up in the air and said, "Any ideas, Bash?" She moved closer to me and did a little jump.

"A walk?"

Closer. Jump. She trailed me outside and down the front steps, almost falling. How much longer Basia can make those legs work for her remains a speculation, which wavers each day. I do not want to guess how much longer she will be able to accompany me on my walks. I need Basia now more than ever, it seems.

We hadn't gone very far before Basia turned around, heading for home. I walked her home, let her back into the house, yelled out to Gemma that I was going farther on my own, and headed back out.

The images of Tanya and Emma embracing with an ardor had almost faded. I was closing in on relief, the tension I experience when I see Emma run and throw herself into Tanya's arms, screaming, "Mama!" had just about been flushed out by my heavy breathing and sweat from my fast-paced walking. Each time I see them go through their passionate greeting, my discomfort becomes less potent. It takes practice, this acceptance. It takes grand and sincere effort to talk myself out of all these feelings that stop everyone from being free to love each other in my presence. I know now that if I cannot stand to watch Tanya and Emma embrace joyfully, then I must turn away or not be there at all, not until it no longer affects me as it still threatens to do sometimes, as it did just this past winter:

Emma and I are cross-country skiing. A gorgeous new snow has left the apple orchard across the road from us, ripe for our trail-breaking skis, me leading the way to make it easier for Emma. The snow is too deep for Basia, so we have to leave her behind, much to her disappointment.

Emma is fairly new to this form of winter exercise. She still has wobbly novice legs and nervous anticipation of falling, which causes her to sit down when she thinks she may be about to. I break trail and we make it into the orchard, which, by now, with the snow still falling lightly, has become a lacy brocade of the cleanest white coating. We are jubilant, laughing, and throwing snow at each other as we go further down toward deeper woods. I want to go and go, on and on into the places where we might encounter deer or fox or coyote, but Emma is getting tired. We have turned around to head home, an upslope battle ahead. I know that I will come back out later but I am still agitated at Emma's growing whiny protestations about how hard this return trip has become for her. I encourage her for a little while until she lies down, refusing to get up.

"C'mon, Emma. We don't have that far to go. You can do it."

"No, I can't!" she yells, her face planted in a small drift.

"Emma! Let's go."

"No!"

Does she cry out for her mama like she did a few years ago on another snowy slope? No. But somewhere in me I can hear and see and smell the rage of all the times Emma has cried out for Tanya, when I was either asking her to do something hard or refusing to do something she wanted me to do. I am beginning to get angry just because I have to wait for her, because my life would be so much easier if Emma wasn't here right now and I could simply go on into deeper woods. I am angry about all the times I have had to struggle with Emma, slamming through my own impatience and intolerance in order to help her move on.

I am so tempted to leave her here, to ski away and leave her to the elements. I swing around and look off into the white, forgiving landscape, trying to come back up to a place of reason and calm. I do not want to continue with this descent into uncontrolled mania over feelings I have worked so hard to reconcile. Cooler, cooler still, the snow certainly is the right temperature and consistency to soothe my flaming senses. But then, Emma speaks and the words only serve to provoke the beast, which was just about to roll over and play dead.

"Why don't you like my mom?" she asks. Did she pick up on what I was struggling with while she was lying face down in the snow? How in the world did she know?

"I don't dislike your mom, Emma. I don't like things about her. And so should you. Why don't you ever get mad at her?" I just can't help myself from diving in.

"I'm not mad at her, that's all."

"Well then, who are you mad at? Because you sure seem mad at someone sometimes."

"No one."

"Why aren't you mad at Tanya?"

"I'm just not, OK?"

"Your mother is an asshole. Don't you want to know anything about her and about what she's done?"

"NO! Stop talking about her!"

"No. Why should I? You never hear the truth about her. You think that it's fair to Gigi and me? Do you know how hard it is to watch you when Tanya shows up and you go running into her arms like she's your hero? She's a jerk and she winds up getting the best of you. She doesn't deserve it." By now, I'm in quicksand up to my waist and it's swallowing me whole. If I don't stop, I will disappear into the bowels of the earth, where I obviously belong.

"Stop talking about her, Kiki!" Emma screams this out into the quiet of the snow. The sound slaps me full bore in my guts. I look at her face. Snow and tears are forming a mushy mix of slush, mostly just below her mouth and nose. What finally gets me to snap out of this fever? I'm not sure but I instinctually go to her and begin taking her skis off. I push down on the release clasps and set her small feet loose.

"Get on my back and I'll carry you home. OK?"

"NO! I'll walk." She starts to pick up her poles and skis but slips, the equipment and her body falling into a scattered splayed mess at my feet. She tries again, without success, to gather things up into her arms. Finally, she sits down, defeated.

I kneel with my back to her, hoping she'll climb aboard.

"I'm sorry, Emma. Please let me carry you home."

Slowly, she crawls toward me. I feel her gloved hands reaching my back and inching up to my shoulders. I wait until she is securely fastened to me, arms and legs wrapped around my body. Then I pick up her gear, adding my own to hers. It's an awkward shuffle through the orchard, across the field to the road and, finally, into our snowy yard. We are silent the entire way home.

"Want some hot chocolate?" I ask quietly once we get inside.

"Yes, please."

Gemma and Basia wander into the room, eager for the outdoor report.

"You OK?" Gemma asks both of us.

I nod, watching Emma, wondering what she will do or say.

"Yep," she replies.

"Did you have a good time?" Gemma asks her directly.

"Yep."

"You sure?" Gemma is beginning to dig.

"Yep." This is as far as Emma will let Gemma go.

I make all of us some hot chocolate, even Basia, who gets a taste in her bowl. I am hoping that it is perfect hot chocolate, perfectly sweet, perfectly warm and perfectly chocolate. I'm hoping it's the best hot chocolate that Emma has ever had and that it helps her to know how sorry I really am. I'm hoping that with every sip, she can forgive me just a little bit more.

I am standing at the foot of Emma's bed, after making it. The shiny magenta coverlet bounces light back at me—pillows fluffed, stuffed animals lined up in official welcoming position. With her room cleaned and vacuumed, we are ready for her to come home. And this is where I want her: safe, messy, flashing her blue eyes in all directions at once—here, in our sage-green house across from an apple orchard, facing east toward a ridge of pines. I want her here in summer, the long days giving her more time to do everything she must do. But even with the hours stretching out in front of her, Emma will end her days wanting more time: her dolls won't be properly dressed—the drawing will need another color—the fairy house has got to have at least three more rooms to accommodate the guests who are arriving for the ball at midnight.

I hear a car door shutting in the driveway, then the rapid prance of Emma's feet on the stone steps.

"Gigi! Kiki! Basia!" she yells as she opens the front door.

The three of us reach the dining room together. Not sure which one of us she should hug first, Emma stops in mid-leap. We move toward her and the four of us huddle up. Tanya comes in from behind Emma. She stops, too, watching from the open door. For a few seconds, I am tempted to bring her into the embrace, but I don't. Tanya remains standing apart from us, watching and smiling with, what I hope is some kind of happiness, as painful as this must be.

"Did you have a good time?" Gemma asks Emma once she raises her face to us.

"Yep." As she says this, she jumps into my arms. Still a featherweight but longer by what seems to be inches, I hold her easily.

"We really missed you," I whisper into her ear. By the way Emma looks at me, I am sure that she believes me.

16

YOU WOULD THINK
BY NOW . . .

Dear Gemma,

Inside of me right now, there is a holy war taking place, one that keeps me distant and sad. This feels like life or death—like really surrendering to life and love with you and Emma or not—every day I get closer to knowing in my bones that this is where I want to be— every day, voices and other parts of me try to convince me that I am not capable of it—that I am a liar and a snake—you have struggles, Gemma—they may not look or sound the same as mine but I know you have them—the thing is, I feel that you are SO judgmental of mine—that every time I try to tell you just how serious this feels to me, you attack me and all I can do is make up stupid excuses, defending myself uselessly— while you were gone, I was totally responsible and I was glad to do it—my transgression does not negate that— it shouldn't alter that fact nor should it diminish your trust in me—

I am fighting for my life here—my life as an honest, sober, responsible, and present participant and partner—you would think by now that I would have been through all of this—left this ridiculous turbulence behind—I cannot explain it—I can only promise that I am on the edge, ready to fall, ready to fly—

Love, the only way I know how,
CarolO

This new therapist is looking at me with a mixture of politically correct New Age interest and old school reproach. I suppose she thinks it is an effective technique, having used it on hundreds of clients before me. She reminds me a bit of Cindy, the social worker who interviewed Gemma and me during the adoption process, except this therapist seems more jaded, or perhaps, skeptical. I promised Gemma that I would start individual therapy before she made the commitment to go to couples counseling. Well, here I am. Another therapist, this one recommended by a friend because she is supposed to have experience with adult substance abusers. How many therapists does this make? We're closing in on an even dozen. I'm beginning to feel that therapy, as valuable as it can be to unlock emotions that have been jammed into the body and then turned into destructive patterns of behavior, can become just as much of an escape as denial or unrealistic rationalization. As long as I am in therapy and "working on myself" then, basically, anything goes. Once in therapy, bad behavior is simply a part of the process. "All these feelings are coming up now that I'm in therapy. We're working on this issue in therapy.

I'm sorry that I'm behaving this way. It must be because I'm in therapy."

"Oh, OK. No problem."

"So, can you tell me why you began drinking again?" Obviously, this therapist wants to get right to the heart of the matter.

"I suppose it's because I like it." I'm not sure why I chose a smart-ass response. Maybe it's the condescending look on her face.

"Yeah. OK. Any other reason?" She is not put off. I know that she wants me to say it helps me escape.

"It helps me escape," I play along.

"From what exactly?"

"Oh, I guess from my responsibilities—taking care of Emma, being a parent, working with kids who have autism, Gemma, the house, chores. Y'know, the usual." The list just has to impress her.

"Well, everyone has a unique set of obligations that they must show up for. I wouldn't say it's 'the usual' in your case. This situation of raising your partner's niece is not usual. How does it make you feel?" Which "it" does she mean? There are a lot of possible "its" here.

"What? Raising Emma?"

"Yes. How does that responsibility make you feel?" Oh, that one.

"All kinds of things. I mean, it's a mix." Seems apparent to me.

"Is it all good, all bad?" Didn't she hear me? It's a mix.

"Neither. I love her, Emma. She's a great kid. Honestly."

"I believe she is but that is not what I'm asking you. I'm trying to get back to the cause of your drinking and why your marriage is at risk. I'm wondering about the feelings you get when you are asked to do something or take care of Emma when you don't want to. You were in a relationship with Gemma for twelve years before Emma came along. That's a huge shift for you and Gemma."

OK. OK. So I know where this is going and, sure, I'll keep playing along. Might as well. We've got another forty-five minutes.

"Well, yeah. I was resentful, I guess, at first. I still am resentful sometimes, but that's to be expected." Isn't it?

"How long do you suppose this resentment is to be 'expected'?"

"I don't know. I'm not sure there is a time limit for these things."

"How often do you get resentful?"

"I honestly don't know. I haven't been keeping track of the exact number."

"When did the drinking start again?"

"Over a year ago now."

"When did you make an agreement with Gemma to stop drinking and go into therapy?"

"A while ago."

"Why has it taken you this long to make an appointment with someone?"

"I'm not sure."

"Do you really want to stop drinking?"

Oh dear. There is no longer any look of New Age fondness or compassion in her eyes. She's already running out of patience with this line of baloney. I try to appear as though I'm in a state of deep consideration, but if I was truly desirous of an end to my drinking, wouldn't my response have been a lightning quick, "Yes! Of course!"

"Well, yes. I am," I finally answer.

"When you have made an honest commitment to stop drinking, give me a call and we'll set up an appointment to continue, if you want. All right?" She stands up, opens the door, and holds out two business cards. Wait a minute. The hour is not up. What is she doing?

She waits with her hand on the doorknob, looking at me without flinching. I slowly get up and walk out of the room, taking the cards as I pass her, a feeling of relieved chagrin spreading throughout my entire body.

"Good luck," she says as she closes the door behind me.

Good luck? That's it? And what kind of luck are we speaking about here? The kind that alcoholics need to thwart the demons of addiction? The kind of luck that assists couples who are in marital trouble? The kind that busts open the heart so it can finally move forward into a new place of acceptance?

I am standing in the hallway in front of the door to the therapist's office. The door has been closed now for about a minute. I cannot move. I want to knock on the door and ask this therapist what she meant by "Good luck." I want to know how she was able to cut me off so easily without any clear way back. I am not used to this type of quick dismissal complete with a caveat for calling her again. It feels like an ultimatum to me. Not even Gemma has threatened me with one of those, at least not as seemingly final and decisive as this one, and after only thirty minutes, too.

I don't knock. I have a feeling that this therapist would simply look at me without much sympathy and reiterate her offer and its conditions. I stand for another couple of seconds before walking down the hall and out to my car. Maybe if I sit quietly for a while, I will come to a place of action—a place of next moves. I turn on some music—the CD I put in a little over an hour ago doesn't fit my mood any longer: *Spring Awakening*. It's the sound track from the Broadway musical about repressed youth and suicide. For God's sake, she didn't even ask me if I was suicidal or if I needed rehabilitation treatment. What kind of a therapist is she anyway? I didn't even get to mention that I've recently been diagnosed with attention deficit disorder and am now taking medication and that drinking is a way to calm my brain, that it helps me turn off the scattered chatter.

I'm starting to get angry. It's better than feeling sorry for myself. It's her problem, not mine. She's a bum therapist, that's what. That's all. She's the kind of therapist who practices tough love. OK. Now I get it. Show the patient to the door. Kick your child out into the cold, then stand back and watch them fall and squirm and fall again, until they somehow get back up, all on their own, or come crawling back, willing to follow orders from tough love therapists. This therapist can go jump.

Then I remember the business cards that she handed to me on my way out the door. I don't remember putting them anywhere though. They must be in a pocket. Yup. There they are, tucked into one of my back pockets, already on their way to becoming wrinkled, unreadable castaways. One is the therapist's card; I won't need that one again. The other card is for a program called, Starting Now, an outpatient drug and alcohol addiction treatment program, which is located right in front of me in the mental health complex that I have just come out of, the same complex where the tough-love therapist has her office.

I am about to throw this card into the backseat of my car, along with the therapist's card, but something stops me. It wouldn't hurt to find out what the program is about. At least I will have proof of my intention to deal with my drinking "problem."

On the way home, I stop and buy a six-pack of beer. By the time I get there, I am ready for questioning.

The house is a dark cell of control issues and big deals. The kid. The adult. The dog. They want the ingredients of compliance and no questions asked. Just listen and nod. There is a broken promise, something they're saying I had agreed to. I thought I was supposed to be enthused about something. What was it? I'm too high to remember.

I opened the door to the house and I entered the dark zone of control, where voices spit out the trail mix of their logic. I'm confused. I thought I was supposed to be grilled about the appointment with the new therapist. I was ready to be grilled. But now they are asking me about some trip to the shore, some trip I was supposed to be a chaperone for. Didn't I tell them I would go? That I would be happy to go? Wasn't that what everyone wanted me to say?

But no. They wanted me to say I didn't want to go so then it would be easier to beg out of the trip altogether. Is that right? So we could say to the other parents that we are not going and then we won't have to secure the drivers, the sleeping arrangements, and the money. So, there is this school trip. Somehow we all came at this trip from different angles. Pushed toward the trip, I thought, I had arranged my equilibrium so I was all set and ready to get into a car with other parents and other kids. I was ready to go out into the ocean even, to watch whales. I get home and that is not what they wanted at all.

I say, "It's not a big deal."

"Yes, it is a big deal, Carol. Don't you remember we talked about this the other day? I wanted you to tell the other parents that we weren't going. Now I have to do it. This is just great. I give you one thing to do and you forget." She stomps off to call the parent who is the coordinator of the class trip.

It really isn't a big deal or is it? I'm so high I can't decide.

There is the sound of engines and humming electrical appliances all up and down the skies. The horizon is blinking on and off with lights from distant barbeques. Emma and Gemma are not home. Gemma is with Don, who has begun the process of dying from cancer. Emma is off to a friend's house for a birthday sleepover party—a ten-year-old girl's dream party: a house filled with girls. For a night, she gets to feel like a part of a pack. This empty house was unexpected—across the hills behind me, comes the approaching pulse of thunder. This, I can handle, no problem. Storms and a dog who has never understood what thunder and lightning are. She beats the floors down with her pacing: back and forth across the maple boards, her nails begin to tap out the rhythm of her anxiety. This I can handle, too. Just a storm and a dog. This is not a storm, a dog, a child, and a wife.

Responsibility for more than just a dog and storm has an exponential growth curve. With just a few more elements (namely, Gemma and Emma) and it's out of control—it tips over into the stagnant reaches of mud—the air so thick with calamity and extreme self-doubt. Weighed down with the thoughts of obligatory tasks and concerns, I cannot move. When they all need something from me, who do I tend to first? Who needs me more? I would go straight for the dog, if I had my so-called druthers. But the heaped plate begs for a different choice. Looks like it will have to be Emma. But wait. Gemma is foaming at the mouth. Gotta lift her up first.

The dog is shaking. She's about to pee on her bed. Wait, wait. Isn't that Emma crying in the other room? No. She's not here. Tonight, it is just a dog and a storm. I am ready to go out for some beer. No one is here to answer to. Storm and dog. No breath detectors or lie detectors. This must be a gift from Bacchus.

I sit on the porch in the rocking chair, listening to the rain and thunder, debating whether I should get the beer or not.

Gemma is standing across the kitchen chopping block from me. "Did you drink while I was away? The night that Emma got back from her sleepover?"

Mmmmm. Let me think here. Best answer would be? This can't be happening. Seriously. It can't be this awful. Emma. Gemma. Basia. Whom am I running from exactly?

"Uh, I uh . . . I uh . . ." I crumble.

Gemma looks at me without giving anything away. A direct hit is coming. My chest muscles pull in tight. I squeak out, "Yeah. I did. Just a couple of beers the other night when Emma was already asleep." I stand at the chopping block, waiting for my sentence and punishment. It doesn't come. Gemma just nods and walks away. Oh my God. Oh my God. What does this mean? I find out the next day when Gemma wraps her words into a great ball of fire and throws it at my head.

"So, I just want to tell you that I'm done. I will not be your drinking monitor anymore. Go ahead and drink. Drink yourself to death if you want to. Don't drink. I'm done. You are on your own. Just promise me that you won't put Emma at risk. OK?"

My brain is burning. What? Where's the slice? Where's the twisting knife? The reprimand?

"All right. OK." I fumble.

"I'm not asking you anymore. Got that?"

"Yup."

"I don't understand why you are choosing to do this to yourself. I don't think I will ever understand why you are drinking again, but it's your choice and I don't want to hear about it anymore. If I find out that you put Emma at risk, I will leave you. You got that?"

"Yup."

It's now or never. That's what Joe from the Alcohol Rehabilitation Program says. I'm not sure I would put it that way but he can say whatever he wants. I'm thinking he can sense how tired of this I am and he can probably imagine how exasperated my family must be by now, after two years of dancing with this demanding partner of mine, namely alcohol, it would only seem obvious that I would give her the heave. She won't let go as easily as all that and so here I am, still twirling around with her in the middle of the dance floor even though the music has stopped, the guests have all left, and the crepe paper decorations have become wrinkled and torn. The dance hall reeks of stale sweat and patchouli oil. It's time to go but I can't seem to leave.

Joe looks me right in the eye, the left one, I think, and asks if I think this kind of program will work for me. Two nights a week, three-hour sessions, for ten weeks, lots of talking, and all the coffee I can drink. In all honesty, I tell Joe I'm not sure. The hours will be practically impossible for me. I've got a wife, a kid, and a dog. School planning time, exercise time, and everything in between. It's too much of a time constraint and to be even more honest, I just don't think any kind of program where I have to sit around with a bunch of drunks is going to help at this point. Why? Isn't that what you are? Well, yeah, but. But what? Too good for them, are you? Well, no, but. But nothing. You do it or you don't. OK. I see. I'll choose, I don't. Call me if you change your mind. Not likely, Joe. Sorry.

Bugger off. Bugger off. Bugger off. No more buggering off for you, babe.

I wish I could say that the struggle with alcohol was over and done. I wish I could say that Gemma's, "Good luck and Good night" speech set me on the straight and narrow. If I could say it, I'd have you believe that just the sight of Emma's face as she smiles at me (at least once a day currently), was enough to make me quit. But I can't say any of these things.

There is still this back and forth thing—off and on—to and fro. But have no pity. Waste not a moment of concern. This is mine: therapists, program directors, and higher powers remain peering in at the windows which face east over the apple orchard where I have gone to look for signs of deer: fallen apples, partially gnawed, hoof prints marked deep into soft spring mud, and small deer pellets, sprinkled down into piles. There are other things that I have found there, even though I was not looking for them: bird feathers, winter berries, lichen, mosses, and once, moose tracks. Whatever I have to do to stop drinking and become present again for everything and everyone I might find when I'm not looking, it must come from within me—while I walk, write, explore, or sit by the brook on a day when there is nothing expected of me. No therapist can tell me what it is I already know: I want to be free and alone. But once upon a time, I made a choice to love another person: Gemma. Love like this doesn't come with free and alone. It doesn't come on my terms only. Every loss and burden has made me want freedom even more. I didn't want a child because it would break me open, setting me up for the kind of pain I never wanted to experience again. But dear, reluctant, CarolO, it's a little too late for that, don't you think?

I did not sign up for the Alcohol Rehabilitation Program. I went to one more therapist who was not of the "tough love" breed. Just when we were ready to stop talking and try some kind of alternate visceral technique that might get past my intellectual sideswiping avoidance, she stopped taking insurance. Oh well.

It's now or never. Those words blast dents in my cranium. Why can't it be sometimes or sometimes? The closer I get to the truth of what I need to do, the farther away it seems. Step up to the plate, Carol. Grow up! Looking east toward the ridge, the sun is rising like a gold locket, inside a promise of life, a collage of photographs from every place I have ever been and of every person I have ever known. I can promise one thing: there will be no happy ending. There will be happy, at times and there will be a moving forward, always learning as I go. But there will never be a conclusion or resolution to the path I am on. I will continue to walk the apple orchard, looking for signs of deer and finding other signs. These will lead me farther on, to places undiscovered and to feelings I have never experienced. Life, for me, is this: the promise of what is to come, reflected back at me from the moments when I was fully present.

17
WATCHING EMMA

S he is waving at me from the field, her thin arm impossible to miss. Those loco motions are Emma-specific; I would recognize them anywhere, as they say. And that said, I feel honored that she is waving at me before the school Fun Run. Right here, from my place as spectator and parent, I have one purpose, one only, to cheer for Emma. She needs to be able to look toward the spot where I am standing and find me here throughout the duration of this one and a half mile after-school wellness event.

For a long time into those first years of taking care of Emma, before the decision to adopt rose up from the well of necessity, I did not enjoy attending the majority of the school functions that Emma was required or wanted to participate in. As a teacher, a certain number of musical functions and sports events are mandated. Throughout my twenty-five years as an educator, I have been to many of them; my cup runneth over with memories of spring concerts where half the kids couldn't hold a note or of soccer games where lots of the points scored were because some kid kicked the ball into their own goal. I've cheered. I've applauded. I've coordinated the ranks, read riot acts in a very stern voice accompanied by the "look," and I've cleaned many a pot after the never-ending stream of pot-lucks. There is a different kind of support that comes with being a parent, as if it weren't obvious, right? With every wave, cheer, or nod, comes the demand for true grit and true intention. It is extremely hard to fake enthusiasm when the kid comes home with you, full of joy and the desire to relive every play, scene. or song with you. Unless you are able to really participate, eyes and ears wide open to your child's every move, your kid will sense that you were not paying attention and the results are certainly not for the faint of heart or the sincere of heart for that matter.

I don't want to be a "perhaps" parent, someone who might be interested or could be counted on, if the time and mood are right. Three years? Four years? Five? It sure seems that I have been struggling to reach this place for way too long. Resistance manifested in so many of my actions and reactions, reaching the point where I almost lost Gemma, Emma, Basia, my home, and my life. I have come as close as I thought I could ever get to resignation and farewell to the people and world that I love. And I could lose it all yet. But somehow, I have arrived here, on this patch of grass, where I am waving with the total conviction of my love for this young girl, who has become my responsibility to protect, encourage, and then send on her way. I cannot tell you how any of this happened. I can only tell the story. Somewhere, within the words, lies the answer to how. I watch Emma and the rest of the runners take off as the Fun Run begins. She is quick at the gate, leaping up like a yearling deer, light and effortless, the spring in her step invisible to the eye. I watch in awe of her, so perfectly gorgeous and fluid as she runs into the wind of this spring day. I do not understand how I got here., parent to this uncoiling pre-adolescent who, by now, has vanished into a flash of white-hot sunlight.

I am now in the role of teacher at the elementary school which Emma attends. I work primarily with first through fourth graders and sporadically in a fifth grade class, one of two and the one Emma is not in. But on two days a week, I am math support teacher in her class, moving from kid to kid, assisting those who don't get it and acknowledging those who do.

I was wary of this arrangement, fearing that Emma might be embarrassed or overly aware of my presence. I was also concerned that I would treat her differently, offering assistance when it wasn't necessary, furnishing her with answers—in other words—giving her an unfair advantage. That has not happened, thankfully. I keep my distance, letting Emma reach for me, if she needs to. For the most part, she has shown remarkably mature restraint, only flying into my arms a handful of times. The second time she did it, I was not prepared and she jumped up fast, banging into my lower jaw with her head which caused me to bite down on my lower lip which began to bleed furiously.

"I'm so glad you're happy to see me, Emma, but could you be a little less enthusiastic next time?" I asked her through my wounded mouth.

Her eyes filled up with tears. I thought that she might begin to sob right there in the cafeteria, but she held it together long enough for me to say, "It's OK. It's not that bad. If I had lost a tooth or two, then it would've been serious, children." I sometimes call Emma, "children." I don't remember how that got started. Emma used to smile when I said it but its charm is wearing off. She looked at me with a frowning glare, the tears disappearing, which was my intention. She hooked arms with a girlfriend and off they went, back to their lunch table.

The only times I show up in her classroom unannounced, are when I am checking up on her for a very specific reason, like the potential of a looming illness or emotional fallout. In those moments, I simply stand at the entrance of the class and watch her, looking for signs of wear or discomfort. A thumbs-up or down from her teacher and we're good to continue with the day. If Emma happens to see me, she usually gives me a little wave or smile. Thus reassured, I can leave without further worry.

Twice, Emma has followed me out of the room for a brief consultation or reassurance session. Both times she needed to talk about an incident that happened on the playground during recess. These half and hour break times seem to either bring out the playfulness or the nastiness in many of the students. It is on the fields, the playground equipment, or the basketball court that the conflicts between kids often come to blows, sometimes literally. Apparently, some crummy behaviors in children do not change over time; I am often surprised that I expected otherwise. Conflicts between children still arise from the same kinds of places that they always have: fear, bigotry, and ignorance. We educator types are consistently trying to figure out new ways of approaching and solving issues that plague schools, those hallowed halls where a free and public education is supposed to be gotten by every student who walks through the front door. We try. But the issues that hound us from the inside out are perpetual, fed by beliefs that are very difficult to change. Here, in our small Vermont hamlet, prejudices and old habits run deep. Steeped in a white, Yankee culture, we struggle to grow up and out from under those attitudes that keep us stuck—it is hard going at times. Most folks certainly do not want to be beaten over the head with our truths, certainly not with my truth.

Only a few parents know that I'm gay. Among the staff, I'd say half are aware that I am married to a woman. I don't keep this fact a secret, but I don't make any grand announcements either. On my desk sits a photograph of Gemma, looking gorgeous and ten years younger. If a student asks, which has not happened yet, I will answer, "She's my partner." What that means to them, I have no idea and, in a way, it's a cop-out. I cannot bring myself to say, "She's my wife" or "She's my great love." What the response would be scares me because I'm sure that many of them would have a problem with it, a problem that they would take home to their parents. I would wager that three quarters of the parent population wouldn't blink an eye but the other one quarter might get stuck with their eyes twitching around in their sockets, unable to put the information in a zone of "Who cares?" I hate that I hold back my response when a child asks, "Are you married?" or "What is your husband's name?" The answers I wind up giving are short, "Yes." "I don't have a husband." If they pursue this line of questioning, I must make an instant judgment—on the defense, in protection mode, I search for an answer that will either deflect or redirect their energy of inquiry. "I don't like talking about my personal life." Why? Why don't I? Wouldn't this be one of those "opportunities" to teach them about tolerance and acceptance? Isn't this the only way things will ever change? Of course. But I'm not always ready for the good fight. I've been through it before, in a little liberal school on a hill, where I thought tolerance ruled the day. Much to my disheartened disbelief, it didn't.

It was the late nineties. We were a small staff of ten. I was teaching the fifth and sixth graders. I was teaching them all about puberty—the body changes, the emotional upheavals and social pressures that come with this time of beginning to figure out sexual identities. Hypocritical in the extreme was my lack of honesty about my lifestyle, which might have helped them with their own confusion. After a couple of months, I decided that I wanted to come out to my students. I brought the question to the staff table; what did they think I should do? I listened to one of the women say that she didn't want her kid to be taught by one of "those people." I was sitting right next to her. I turned to her and said, "I am one of 'those people.'" "Well, I know. But, that's different." To this day, I do not understand what she meant by that.

The principal cut us all off at the pass, declaring that it was up to me, she would support me in whatever my decision turned out to be. With the words, "those people" rolling around inside my head, I put a photo of Gemma on my desk, began to speak about her in my everyday references, and waited. Sure enough, the question finally came through from a sweet-natured boy of eleven,

"Who is that?" pointing to the picture.

"That's Gemma, my partner."

"Oh. OK."

His mother approached me a week later. "I just wanted you to know that Marcus came to me with questions about your partner, Gemma. Is it all right if I talk to him about it?" Her face was sincere and soft with concern.

"Sure. I've been trying to figure out a way to let them know without making a big deal of it."

"Well, you have my full support. I think it's great. Let me know if there is anything I can do to help. OK?"

If only all parents were like her. Soon, a number of other parents came to me, offering up their support, one parent going as far as asking for a parent/teacher forum to discuss tolerance/intolerance issues, which I felt was unnecessary. Perhaps I should have agreed to it.

Another parent, of a fifth-grade girl went to our principal, voicing her fear that I had a "gay agenda," perhaps wanting to influence her daughter toward a lesbian way of life. With a calm and level tone, the principal told this parent that I was a professional and would not let my personal life interfere or influence my students in any way, shape, or form. Thank you, Molly. I tried to shake the feelings of unease that this aroused in me for the remainder of the school year. I was always on alert, conscious of statements or touches that could be construed as sexually influential or sexually inappropriate, particularly with the girls. Being affectionate by nature, this was no simple task. I held back. I smiled less. I stopped myself mid-sentence, afraid that my words might be misinterpreted.

That young eleven-year-old girl moved on to another school the following year. I wish I could say that with her went my inhibitions and paranoid thoughts. But these things did not go away—abated perhaps but not totally assuaged.

Presently, a low-riding discomfort with being in a same-sex relationship lives on in me. My approach these days is to answer as honestly as I can when asked. If a kid eventually does ask me who the woman in the photograph is, I'll say that she's Gemma, my partner. I will deal with the repercussions that follow and I am sure that the principal will support me, being a forward-thinking type of guy. I've got to have faith that this educational environment is a safe one for me, Gemma, and Emma. I have to believe that when I hold out my hand to a parent of a new friend that Emma has made, they will not recoil when I say, "I'm Emma's aunt. Gemma and I are raising her." I must trust that shifts in consciousness do happen, even in the most rigid of minds. As Emma continues to run toward me, holding out her arms, urging me to pick her up and hug her fervently, her friends and classmates will be watching. Through that repeated action, acceptance will hopefully be seeded and grow within them. They will take this acceptance home, inadvertently passing it on to their parents. Without realizing it, the hard and hateful opinions that exist within them about lesbians will soften. Minds and hearts will open. Emma will be invited over to their houses. Gemma or I will pick her up and be forced to have a conversation that might not have happened otherwise. We will stand on the sidelines together, watching our children race, sing, or play. We'll exchange parenting tips. We will offer up advice based on experience. We will look past the labels which brand us. We will slowly erase the phrases that only serve to condemn us and keep us separated from each other. In the name of our children, we will hopefully make better choices about how we treat one another, setting those judgments of our differences aside.

As the kids come running to the finish line, we are all clapping, whatever differences that exist, indistinguishable. All I can see are laughing and buoyant faces—a celebration without any thought of persecution, self-righteousness, or reprimand. Here, on this patch of grass, we are united. We are parents, wanting our children to feel good about their accomplishments, which can be as small as having participated in the Fun Run, not necessarily making it to the end. I am standing on the sidelines, shoulder to shoulder with other par-

ents, welcoming Emma into my arms. There is nowhere else
I would rather be: loving Emma and maybe, by doing so,
bringing a small opening of acceptance into the lives of those
who share this world with us as I feel a shift taking place inside
of me as well. Acceptance. Why has it been so hard?

I am sitting in the living room, observing the sunlight as it ac-
centuates the smudge marks left by Basia's snout on the plate-
glass door window. These smudges, photographs, her dog dish,
collar, and half a bag of dog food are all we have left, those
small items, a yard and a house full of her presence. Everywhere I look, there she is—running, lying, wading, eating—
dear Basia—seventeen years of devotion. The images crumble
and fade. How long will those smudges linger on the glass?
How long will her smell rise up out of the vacuum cleaner?

Two months gone, Twirly. I wait for you every morning. In
the front yard, I wait for you, limp and stiff, rocking front to
back, down the slope to me. I wait to walk with you. I wait to
wake up with you. Maybe someday, this waiting will not feel
so excruciating. Maybe I'll realize that waiting will only make
the pain of missing you worse, harder to bear. Maybe someday,
I will be able to wash those smudges from the glass door and
honor you by living fully not by waiting for you when I know
that you will never again meet me at the bottom of our yard.
But not yet.

The hill holds you now. The earth is your home, taking
you back, breaking your tired old body down into essential elements and releasing them. I will think of you this way: always

giving us something essential, what we all need and want most—clear and exuberant love. In this world, there is nothing higher.

Thank you, Basia.

I hope we did right by you.

18
GUESS WHO'S COMING
TO DINNER?

I am sitting at our dining room table, holding hands with Gemma to my left and Gus on my right. He is sitting across from me so our arms must stretch over the bounty of food that awaits us. This is how we give thanks at our house—creating a circle of hands as each one of us says "Thank you" for something important in our lives. Tanya and Gus are here for dinner, the first one since they were married, the first one since Gemma and I adopted Emma.

Tanya has found religion—going to church every Sunday in the small Maine town where she and Gus live now. I certainly have no objections to that. I'd choose baby Jesus over crack cocaine any day. The good news is, she has not become a zealot, who might walk through the door and instantly slam brochures at us, or throw out beatitudes into the thin air of

201

our intolerance. Once in a while, she will say, "I'm praying for Carol." You can't argue with that.

We are all thankful for this gathering, one a long time coming, one each of us was, in some way I'm sure, dreading. By now, Gemma and Emma seem to be on the other side of accepting the situation as it is. I don't know about Tanya and Gus although they appear pretty relaxed—must be Jesus. I'm the holdout—the last one to come around; everyone acts as if they know it, going a bit out of their way to make sure I'm having a good time.

Emma keeps looking over at me, gauging my mood by the expression on my face. She wants all of us to get along, particularly me and Tanya. Throughout the last five years, she has constantly ragged me with the question: "Why don't you like my mom?" The answers I have given vary depending on my state of mind, or rather, the state of Tanya on my mind. "I don't dislike Tanya. I just don't like her." How Emma could make sense of that, who knows and I never try to explain it. It certainly didn't give her much to go on or much to feel reassured about. On several occasions I tried to rise above my stilted state of stasis and say something like, "I like Tanya. I just don't like some of the decisions she has made." And then, of course, there have been the responses that have come straight from the (what Tanya probably considers to be) mouth of Satan himself, so full of evil these responses were. "I hate your mother, if you must know the truth. And so should you. She's a fucking asshole. Why don't you ask her why she wound up in jail? Huh? Why don't you hate her?" There's no way to feel proud about those moments and I am sure hoping that Emma forgives me. Maybe with Tanya's baby Jesus connection, I will be absolved. All I know is, it's been at least a year since I spewed such vitriol at Emma about Tanya; it's long enough to feel secure about sharing a meal with her.

The thanks expressed and acknowledged, we begin eating the elegant meal that Gemma created—she has never failed at it, I swear. There may have been parts of a seven course feast that were not perfectly rendered, but the other parts have always made up for it. Within a few minutes the accolades begin—it sure is true what "they" say about the benefits of breaking bread together. It's a balm. Sit down to a good meal with your enemy and watch the hate fall away. Good food and the act of sharing it with others has always worked to bring together even the bitterest of foes, at least for a short breath of time. Stopped by the human need for taking in nourishment, especially if it's beautifully presented, allows the rifts to be momentarily forgotten. Full focus is transferred to the sensual act of eating—a place of pleasure attained by all participants. There is no room for fighting, bickering, or even thoughts of it. All the senses are directed into the taking in of food, and everything that goes with it: passing of plates, tasting, sipping, wiping, swallowing, smelling, and seeing. I have never been able to eat and fight at the same time. Many a meal has gone untouched if Gemma and I have been arguing right before or during its creation. "I'm not hungry." Who could be when filled with such anger? A palatable energy, rage fills up the body almost as if it had mass.

Sufficiently emptied of my feelings of rage for Tanya, I can now sit at a table with her and actually eat. Progress? I'd say so. The truth is, or let's say, a part of the truth is, Tanya and I are a lot alike and this revelation has been difficult for me to swallow. (Hah!) Admitting this to myself has been paramount to admitting I am an addict loser freak, incapable of taking care of Emma, just the task I'm supposed to be rising to and growing up for. If I'm like Tanya, how can I possibly raise Emma successfully? This whole situation therefore has been a colossal ruse and I am the fake at the helm.

We meet here at the dinner table, two freaks. Looking across at Tanya, I see nothing but an attractive, middle-aged woman, eating a pasta dinner. A fiend? An enemy? A liar and a snake? These are demons that I have conjured, for what reasons, I'm not sure. I cannot think of why she has come toward me as a dark force that I must vanquish or condemn. All of my actions seem to come under the heading of: Self Protection. But protection against what? I did not want a child, this much is true. But is that enough of a reason to hate either Tanya or Emma? What have either of them done to me or taken from me?

Tanya is sitting across from me, unwilling to look me straight in the eyes, afraid of recrimination or expressions that would punish her for abandoning Emma. Wasn't giving Emma to us the right decision? Wasn't that honorable? Who am I to endlessly split her into pieces? She is not beholden to me. If her daughter, an eleven-year-old, can accept and honor her mother for saving her soul, why can't I?

A piece of spaghetti gets stuck in my throat. Oh my God! What in the world have I been doing? A five year siege. The most reluctant of parents I could possibly have been and to what end? I am thinking of all the times I have made Tanya's life miserable: hanging the phone up on her, walking away from her in a cloud of smoky vehemence, standing in silent fury as she walked away with Emma in her arms. Have I made her pay? If so, for what exactly? For the sin of having a child that she could not raise beyond the age of six without bringing harm? Let her go. Let this go. Tanya had enough faith and love inside her that she was able to give her child to Gemma and me to raise. And I, in all my tortured glory, spat back at her with the kind of relish only the truly self-righteous can possess.

Tanya is sitting across from me, eating a well-deserved meal. I want her to walk away satisfied, full, and comforted. I want her to know, deep in her bones, that this circle, created by the five of us sitting here, really does include her, just as she is. I don't want her to beg or grovel anymore. I don't want to punish her any longer. Wherever Tanya had to go inside herself to make the decision that landed Emma on our doorstep five years ago, is a place I have never gone. It was a place of the truest kind of love—Tanya must be honored for this. As I watch her, slightly hunched over her plate of food, I am filled with an overwhelming sense of remorse. The spaghetti suddenly tastes sharp, full of acids and bitter spices. I'm not sure that I can continue eating. The memories of my blind and selfish ways have poisoned this meal. I hope no one else is sensing my internal admission of guilt? I don't want to ruin it for anyone else. OK, Carol, get back to the spaghetti.

Once upon a time it was too much to ask of me. Once upon a time I didn't want a child, screaming out in a ranting fever to lift the responsibility for a young life from me. Once upon a time, I didn't know any better.

It's Sunday morning, Tanya's time to call Emma. As steadily as the gnats that fly into our faces night and day, she calls, promptly: nine a.m. I reach for phone. I want to say good morning to Tanya.

"Mornin'. How's it going, Tanya?"

"Good, Carol. I'm getting ready to go to church. Thought I'd say hey to my girl. Is she up?"

"Not quite. She slept in. Want me to get her up?"

"No. No. Just tell her I called, OK?"

"Sure. What's new?"

"Y'know. Not much. Gus has a new job driving for a trucking company. I'm working at Salvation Army. I heard about your troubles, Carol. Sorry. I'm with ya."

"Thanks." At first, I'm not sure what she's talking about. Then I remember—my relapse. Drinking again. I'm certain that Gemma has talked with her about it.

Tanya, probably more than just about anyone else, would be able to understand the concept of relapse after fifteen years of sobriety.

"I get it, Carol. Don't give yourself a hard time, OK? I love ya, girl. Tell Emma to give me a call if she wants to."

Here in the world of addict/loser/freak, we forgive each other our transgressions. Not a whole lot of processing needed. Relapse? Got it. Recovery? Maybe. Jesus? Why not?

In a few weeks, Gemma, Emma, and I are traveling to Maine for Thanksgiving. We will stay at Tanya and Gus's house. We'll have Thanksgiving dinner with the entire family. It will probably stretch before us, long into the afternoon, light settling over the lake that the house looks out toward. We'll give thanks again, our view of the world influenced by all our losses and all our gains. On this Thanksgiving, Don is no longer with us, neither is Basia, both of them dying within a month of each other. Grief will be shared—everyone at the table will be able to say, "I am sad, heartbroken even, learning to go on in spite of the pain the death of loved ones brings. But I am thankful, too. I am thankful for the expanse beyond this house on the lake. I am thankful that we can come together, not always united in beliefs but always united in the desire to do the right things for those we love. Let's fill up on turkey, potatoes, brussel sprouts, rolls, yams, cranberry sauce, and pumpkin pie with ice cream, not anger and fear."

19
A Day in the Life

*U*p and at them! The radio goes off at six a.m. and I
promptly fall back to sleep. Forty-five minutes later
and I wake from a dream that I was having about pancakes. I
want one badly, but there is no time for making pancakes or
anything else for that matter. I have just enough time to make
my two cups of coffee (one for my travel mug), take a shower,
grab my gear for the day, and get going to school. I have a
meeting to show up for—a parent/teacher conference. I know
that I'm going to be late; what else is new? Since my father's
death two months earlier, I am plagued with a sadness that
takes all my dreaming energy. Sleep does not offer the kind of
rest it once did and I wake up exhausted. If anyone at school
is upset with me for my almost predictable delays, they have

not said anything, but I know that this has got to change. My excuses are no more reasonable than anyone else's.

I used to be a morning person, able to spring up and out even in the dark wee hours of the day. These days, once I get cracking, I am an on-fire kind of gal but the waking thing is hard. Basia was always an effective motivator; I knew that she needed me in order to get her day started, especially as her senses began to play tricks on her. With her and my father gone, I have less reason to rise. Give me sleep and the mist of dreams. Waking up to the silence that Basia's absence has created and to the daily re-awareness of my father's death, only serves to send me back to the land of unconsciousness. Beyond the silence comes the jam-packed day—sometimes starting with getting Emma out of bed—a formidable task and a constant lesson in the fine practice of detachment.

Emma seems to be coming back from the depths of the ocean each morning; maybe all pre-teens wake up this way. We have tried lots of different ways to get her up, from gently stroking her arms to an alarm clock that plays bird calls. My favorite is the rooster because it is so loud and invasive, but Emma has slept through it more than once. If Gemma and I can get her past the initial arousal stage, straight through to up and at them (them being her clothes, hairbrush, toothbrush, vitamins, and her backpack filled with books and papers), then she usually leaves the house in a good mood. But if she gets stuck getting at "them," her mood might wind up in the realm of foul. Stand back and take cover if you know what's good for you.

Sometimes the three of us are in the land of foul together. Not good. With me in racing-off-I'm-late-for-another-meeting mode, Gemma in would-you-both-stop-whining-and-get-out-of-here mode, and Emma in leave-me-alone mode, I'm certain the sparks are flying. The family talks, the cajoling, bribing, tricks, and ploys have failed for the most part. And so, it remains a crap shoot—the roll of the dice and the roll of the hormones determining our morning fate.

Picture it: Three melodramatic and moody babes together under one roof. The oldest (me) in the final throes of menopause, the next in line (Gemma) at the opening ceremonies of menopause, and the youngest (Emma) heading straight into puberty. Basia, nearing one hundred and nineteen in dog years when she died two months ago in the fall, was the sanest of the bunch. With our dukes up, our hair standing on end, and our eyes flashing bolts of white fire at each other, it's truly a miracle we leave the house alive every day.

Work and school seem to have a calming, if not, exhausting effect on all of us. After a day on the job as a special education teacher, working with kids that have all kinds of issues, from broad emotional to specific learning disabilities, I come home ready for a hot tub soak. But we don't have a hot tub. Running around the school, putting out fires, instructing kids in the ways of reading, writing, and arithmetic is like jumping around in a barnyard while being shot at with a BB gun, trying to pop popcorn. Kind of perfect for me.

Gemma answers every conceivable question from the second-hand store shopping masses three days a week. Running a recycled merchandise shop to raise money for Hospice, allows her strengths to be put to the greatest of ends. At "the Shop," Gemma coordinates, negotiates, mediates, dictates, and decorates—all things that she exceeds at. It drains her dry sometimes—her fragile immune system fending off invasive energy for just so long before the retreat and collapse. She comes home ready for bed and the kind of sleep that will rejuvenate her, the kind of sleep she only rarely enjoys.

Emma is at school from eight a.m. to three p.m. every weekday—fifth grade. Socially, she is in her element: the world of friends—the sun, the moon, the stars, and the universe beyond. If she can focus on school work, such as math, reading, and writing, she holds her own, receiving generally average to above average for grades. Although Emma asks about her grades and will begrudgingly talk about her academic performance, it really isn't what motivates her. Friends and creativity, all spicy and hot, have her claimed.

When she gets home, Emma is ready to call a friend, draw a picture, and create a new piece of furniture for a doll, talk to anyone, including herself, or play with anything she can find. No matter what she does, it will be with the energy of a dervish, the kind that ceaselessly whirls. Her spinning usually reaches a crescendo just before she goes to sleep, but not always. One night recently, the peak came earlier, with a frantic sprint to the finish. This was unlike her. Watching from the wings, Gemma and I looked on with deepening concern; what was she doing? Finally, she crumpled, exhausted and confused. She didn't understand it either.

It's beginning to look more and more like Emma will not have an easy time with the transition into adolescence. From where I stand, there is no turning back now. We certainly can't stop the hormones from their surging emergence into Emma's bloodstream. Already her moods are running deeper, the urgency and drama of what she is feeling taking over her responses to what we are asking her to do. The stomping march across the dining room floor to her bedroom after the words, "It's not fair," is becoming her way of disengaging from us when the heat is on. Gemma and I have to learn how to give her the room for messy and tumultuous emotions without our interfering need to have her apologize or process them. None of this is fatal, but it sure feels like it sometimes. We have got to find the humor and the acceptance that will help us get through. I am hoping that I have what it takes to do just that.

We are eating, forkful after forkful of standard Thanksgiving fare with a few of Gemma's family traditional dishes added to the mix, such as stuffed onions—wouldn't be my pix but, heck, I'm not one of the cooks or the hostess. Not that I wouldn't or couldn't pull off any one of the offerings which are now gracing the table; I've baked a mean turkey in my day. I even prepared (plucked and stuffed a turkey that had just been slaughtered), baked, and served a turkey dinner when I was a wayfarer in Crete over thirty years ago. But this Thanksgiving, the first one without Don, the patriarch of the family, is being hosted by Tanya, who also did the majority of the cooking, the rest being furnished by Gemma, Kay, Sarah, and Joyce, the in-laws.

It's a jovial group despite the waves of grief that wash in from the lake to the west of this summer vacation house that Tanya and Gus are renting for the winter. With unpredictable angles running every which way, the house throws off your sense of direction, especially at night, when you don't have the lake as a reference. Tanya tells us that just about every section of the house was added on—to what? I want to know. I can't tell which part was the original. Apparently, she can't tell either or wasn't told by the obviously wealthy owners of the place. We make do with the odd angles, being an odd bunch ourselves; it's somehow fitting.

We are rarely all together; as a matter of fact, I'm thinking the only other time this group was together was for a celebration of Don and Kay's fiftieth wedding anniversary, over eight years ago in Florida. Looking around the table at the faces of these people that I know as family but actually know very little about, I can safely say we are doing the best we can under circumstances guaranteed to challenge the strongest of hearts. I don't know these people all that well, this much is true, but I have great love for each one as we share this Thanksgiving meal. We are here together, making room for each other even if it is difficult.

There is Kay, her heart broken by the death of her husband, raising a glass to his memory. Who can make sense of "gone?" There is Tanya, smiling, knowing that her most precious love, her daughter, Emma, will not stay with her when the toasts are over. There is Gemma, loving and questioning the relationship with her partner, me. There is me, being as thankful as I can for this thing called "family."

As I hug Gemma's older brother, Carl, goodbye the next day, he whispers in my ear, "I know you guys are going through a hard time. You're part of our family now. You can't leave us." I look him in the eyes, the sincerity genuine. Maybe he is right. I want to find out.

It's my turn to put Emma to bed tonight. These days, I look forward to it. Almost eleven, Emma still needs us to lie with her until she has really shaken off any thoughts, ideas, or anxieties that are lingering within her mind, causing her to resist falling asleep. Gemma and I have finally given into the fact that she needs this ritual. We tried curing her of it, but she just wasn't ready. I figure that if she isn't over it by the time she is thirteen, all of her friends will be teasing her relentlessly and the shame of it will cause her to ban us from her room. There was a time when we couldn't leave her without a huge crying and pleading scene: "Don't leave me. Don't leave me," she would sob. Now, we can slip away when she is still awake, but drowsy, without her hysterical begging. We take this as clear signs of progress.

After reading to her for half an hour, her breathing slowing way down to a brush stroke of sound, I turn off the light and lightly stroke her back. I tuck my face tight into her hair;

freshly washed, it smells like lemons. My fingers feather out the kind of lullaby that only loving touch can sing. She settles softly down into the bed, so safe and warm and sweet. I almost fall asleep but rouse myself so I won't wind up spending a good portion of the night here. I want my ritual with Gemma now. As I leave the room, I whisper, "Sweet dreams." Emma is awake enough to whisper back, "Sweet dreams, Kiki." We can both rest a little easier now.

20
ELEVEN IT IS

*E*mma turns eleven today. She is not spending it with
Gemma and me. For the first time in six years, she is
spending it with Tanya. I call to sing "Happy Birthday" to
Emma, getting my chipmunk voice ready so she will laugh.
Tanya answers. She sounds so happy. The sound of her happiness used to sting and taunt me. Today, it rustles my nerves
for a couple of moments and then it makes me happy, too.
Mother and daughter, as close as they were for years, can be
close and happy now. I know that when the two of them are
together sometimes, it will still choke the breath out of me.
But it will happen less and less. I am certain of this, if my response today is any indication of how far I have come.

"Thank you so much, Carol, for letting her be here with

me on her birthday," Tanya says. She doesn't need to thank me, but I guess she felt it was important.

I sing to Emma in my best impersonation of Alvin, one of the chipmunks from the movie, *Alvin and the Chipmunks*. She laughs and then immediately starts to describe the Curious George birthday cake that they will be having at her party. For an instant, I cringe with jealousy, really understanding just how much fun she is having with her mom and how important Tanya still is to her. I keep my voice light and cheerful. On her eleventh birthday, my gift to her is letting mother and daughter have their relationship without getting in the way.

"I wish you were here," Emma says. How did she know that I wanted to hear her say something like that?

"Me, too, Honey Lamb. But it sounds like you are having a really great time."

"I am."

"Good."

Emma and I say our good-byes and Tanya gets back on the phone.

"It's so nice to wake up with her here with me on her big day. I usually have a hole in my heart on her birthday," she says.

"Enjoy your daughter, Tanya. You both deserve it."

I hang up the phone and begin to cry. Sometimes there are only these moments of change and acceptance to show for the distance I have come from being that reluctant mother and partner almost six years ago. I cannot predict what will come toward us as we grow older—Gemma and I have been straddling a line, a very narrow stretch of white paint running directly in front of us as we walk on. Past the crisis that my drinking has brought on, we are still wondering whether or not splitting up would be best for everyone. But each night when Gemma moves in close to my body just after I have turned off the light, what stretches out in front of me is the shared softness of sleep, a place I can only go if Gemma is next to me. And each night, I say, "Sweet dreams," to Emma, whether I'm the one reading to her or not. She always responds, with a voice that sounds like a hushed melody of peaceful contentment, "Sweet dreams, Kiki." I bring these small, holy rituals with me every night as I fall asleep, drifting beyond that place of reason, to another place, where I am not resistant to love, especially the love from and for a child. I will hold out for this love; I will look for it in my dreams and I will welcome it in my life, whenever I am able.

EPILOGUE:
RED EFT ON THE ROAD

I am on my bicycle—a dusk ride to shed the day's tension. Speeding down the sloping dirt road, going faster than I should, I see it: a red eft looking west. I ride past it, leaving its survival to fate. Halfway across the road, it stands a fairly good chance of making it all the way over, a car tire unable to turn it dimensionless once it has made it.

Before I get too much farther though, I am slammed by the thought of the red eft's possible death and my contribution to it if I don't help it along. I brake and turn back. There it is—little red eft, head still raised to the west. I get off my bicycle, leaving it lying by the side of the road as I find a large enough leaf to have the newt crawl onto for transport. I place the leaf gently in front of it—the red eft remains motionless, held by its instinctual command: don't move when something large is near. With my fingers, I urge it onto the leaf from behind. It tries to wiggle away, but the leaf is unavoidable. The wiggling simply propels it onto the leaf where it ceases to move.

As quickly as I can, I lift the leaf and newt, taking them to a place across the road into a clump of low small plants, grasses, and twigs. The red eft scrambles off the leaf and away, disappearing into the shadows.

I remain crouched there, smiling after the newt. This little act of grace has set me free to keep going. My way is clear. I will see other red 'efts' that did not make it across the road. I will continue to assist as many as I can. Somehow on this day, it is balancing out. My perceptions of life and death and my relationship with the forces that bind us together seem to be in balance. I can ride on, my mind flashing from one word to another, from one phrase to another, in awe of the brain's capacity for thought. These are my moments of escape: alone, flying, and filled with the presence of my own giddy madness, allowing it to be, without judgment and condemnation. I am human. Fully. No defenses. No need for excuses or contrition or apologies. I am riding my bicycle as fast and hard as I can. I am flying down my old dirt road. I am nowhere else. I am here. This is my place. This is Gemma's place. This is Emma's place. We belong here, in this world together. This is our happy ending: straight on and fist first into the life set so beautifully and mysteriously before us.

ABOUT THE AUTHOR

CAROL A. ORTLIP is a special education teacher who hopes to open I.N.S.P.I.R.E. for Autism, a private school for autistic students, in Guilford, Vermont. The author has held a variety of jobs in her life's journey, from crab fisher in Alaska to hansom cab driver in Manhattan. She is also the author of *We Became Like a Hand: A Story of Five Sisters* (2002), a poignant memoir of family and sisterhood. She lives near Brattleboro, Vermont, with her partner Gemma, Emma, and their new puppies, Sassy and Hugo.

Photo by Barbara Docktor